Global Security & Intelligence Studies

Also from Westphalia Press

westphaliapress.org

Global Security & Intelligence Studies

Volume 1, Number 2
Spring 2016

Edited by
Yoav Gortzak & Patricia J. Campbell

WESTPHALIA PRESS
An imprint of Policy Studies Organization

Volume 1, Number 2 of Global Security and Intelligence Studies
All Rights Reserved © 2017 by Policy Studies Organization

Westphalia Press
An imprint of Policy Studies Organization
1527 New Hampshire Ave., NW
Washington, D.C. 20036
info@ipsonet.org

ISBN-13: 978-1-63391-521-3
ISBN-10: 1-63391-521-2

Cover design by Jeffrey Barnes:
jbarnesbook.design

Daniel Gutierrez-Sandoval, Executive Director
PSO and Westphalia Press

Updated material and comments on this edition
can be found at the Westphalia Press website:
www.westphaliapress.org

Global Security and Intelligence Studies
Volume 1, Number 2 - Spring 2016
© 2016 Policy Studies Organization

Table of Contents

Editorial Welcome

♞

*G*lobal Security and intelligence Studies aims to publish high-quality and original research on contemporary security and intelligence issues. The journal is committed to methodological pluralism, and seeks to help bridge the gap between scholars and practitioners engaged in security and intelligence issues by publishing rigorous research, book reviews, and occasional think pieces that are relevant to both communities. We will, on occasion, also seek to publish special issues on timely intelligence and security topics, and welcome proposals that fit with the scope and aims of the journal. The journal actively encourages both former and current intelligence and security practitioners to participate in important scholarly and policy debate, and invites them to contribute their research to the journal. As a result, we hope that the journal will become a vibrant platform for informed, reasoned, and relevant debates on the most important intelligence and security issues of our time.

This special issue on cybersecurity addresses one such important topic, and offers a variety of perspectives on one of the most important security problems in the contemporary international system. In *Reacting to Cyber Threats: Protection and Security in the Digital Age*, Anthony Craig and Brandon Valeriano offer an empirical assessment of state responses to the advent of offensive cyber capabilities.

In *Arming Cyberspace: The Militarization of a Virtual Domain*, Miguel Gomez argues that while most states are concerned about growing threats from cyberspace, not all states are interested in the militarization of cyberspace. Gomez examines the variation in state responses to cyber threats, by offering an explanation for why some states assign cyber-defense tasks to their military forces, while others rely on civilian organizations to defend themselves against cyber threats. Robert Farley's article, *Intellectual Property, Cyberespionage, and Military Diffusion*, highlights yet another aspect of cybersecurity. It explores the ways in which states, like China, use cyberespionage to obtain intellectual property related to military technology. Cyberespionage directed against defense contractors and others, he finds, is another avenue for the diffusion of military technology in the international system. Finally, Trevor Sutherland's article, *Applying Robert A. Pape's Denial Strategy to Computer Warfare*, explores the applicability of an influential argument about conventional warfare and coercion to cyberspace.

Publishing an academic journal is a collaborative process. The editorial team would like to extend its gratitude to the authors, to our peer reviewers for their feedback and commitment, and the members of the editorial board for their support and input.

On behalf of the editorial team,

Yoav Gortzak
American Public University System

Patricia J. Campbell
American Public University System

doi: 10.18278/gsis.1.2.1

Global Security and Intelligence Studies - Volume 1, Number 2 - Spring 2016

Intellectual Property, Cyber Espionage, and Military Diffusion

Robert Farley[A]

This article investigates the diffusion of military technology through the cyber theft of intellectual property (IP). During the Cold War, both the United States and the Soviet Union worried about illicit appropriation of military technology, some of which occurred through review of IP documents. Recently, these concerns have intensified, as the expanding use of IP has offered a window—sometimes one left wide open—for theft. This is particularly the case for dual-use technology, which is less likely to have been initially created with secrecy protections in place. In recent years, sources have alleged that China is appropriating a vast amount of military-related IP from the United States. As the digital age has matured, there is persuasive evidence that China is taking advantage of the steps involved in others' IP regimes by using cyber espionage to access into materials developed as part of the IP legal regime. These include defense contractors' internal legal documents, law firms' written evaluations of technology, as well as patent applications submitted to the Patent and Trademark Office. The opportunity that these access points provide adds a new layer to the analysis of the diffusion of military technology.

Key words: *military technology, diffusion, cyberespionage, intellectual property, China*

Introduction

Over the summer of 2015, the popular national security blog "Lawfare" asked readers to name the most hackable database operated by the United States government. The request came in the wake of a massive Office of Personnel Management database hack in spring 2015. The primary authors and readers of Lawfare submitted dozens of potential databases, mostly involving various types of information about government personnel.[1]

Two of the databases, however, made a different kind of sense. One, proposed by Ben Wittes, was the Commerce Department's database of export control applications, which determine how and where US firms can export sensitive "dual use" technology.[2]

[A] Lecturer, Patterson School of Diplomacy and International Commerce at the University of Kentucky.
[1] Benjamin Wittes, "Other Unclassified Databases the Chinese Are Probably Stealing," Lawfare, July 27, 2015. https://www.lawfareblog.com/other-unclassified-databases-chinese-are-probably-stealing.
[2] ibid.

doi: 10.18278/gsis.1.2.2

The second, suggested by reader Jonathan Lichtman, was the US Patent and Trademark Office database, which includes applications, with supporting materials, for US patent protection.[3]

Given the long history of suspected and confirmed industrial espionage on the part of the People's Republic of China (PRC), both of these databases would make apt targets. Indeed, the available evidence on Chinese cyber-espionage efforts suggest that the People's Liberation Army (PLA) has focused on US and European intellectual property (IP), with a particular concentration on IP in the defense sector.

This article examines illegitimate diffusion of military technology through the theft of draft patents and trade secrets through cyber warfare. During the Cold War, both the United States and the Soviet Union dealt with concerns about illicit foreign appropriation of military technology, some of which occurred through review of IP documents. In the post-Cold War context, these concerns have intensified, as the expanding use of IP has offered a window—sometimes one left wide open—for theft. This is particularly the case for dual-use technology, which is less likely to have been initially created with secrecy protections in place. In recent years, various sources (including the US government and several private firms) have accused China of appropriating a vast amount of IP from the United States, much of it related to military affairs. Of course, China engages in old-fashioned face-to-face espionage. But as the digital age has matured, there is persuasive evidence that China is taking advantage of the steps involved in others' IP regimes, by using cyber espionage to access into materials developed as part of the IP legal regime. These include defense contractors' internal legal documents, law firms' written evaluations of technology, as well as patent applications submitted to the Patent and Trademark Office. The frequency of attack against these access points suggests that states continue to overlook their significance. The opportunity that these access points provide adds a new layer to the analysis of the diffusion of military technology.

IP and Military Technology

Why concentrate on IP law? Historically, the security studies subfield has paid little attention to development in international or domestic IP law, beyond a comment here or there about how technological innovation requires a sound legal basis.[4] Few studies, however, have focused on how legal foundations affect a military–industrial complex or how the emerging international IP regime might affect the diffusion of military technology.[5]

---

[3] Paul Rosenzweig, and Benjamin Wittes, "Users Weigh in on What Database the PLA Should Hack Next," *Lawfare*, July 31, 2015. https://www.lawfareblog.com/users-weigh-what-database-pla-should-hack-next.

[4] Robert L. Paarlberg, "Knowledge as Power: Science, Military Dominance, and U.S. Security," *International Security* 29 (1) (Summer 2004): 135.

[5] Susan K. Sell, *Private Power, Public Law: The Globalization of Intellectual Property Rights* [Kindle] (Cambridge: Cambridge University Press, 2003).

But there are now several reasons to believe that IP law, both in its domestic development and in the context of the emerging international IP regime, may be having a strong, independent effect on the way states innovate and on how those innovations find their way around the international community.

First, political demands of defense contracting have grown steadily more complex. Arms export agreements have increasingly taken on the character of transnational public–private partnerships. To sell fighter jets, US firms have to agree to build components in the customer country, as well as to transfer technology associated with the weapon system. This creates the need for intricate legal arrangements that delineate where and how firms can transfer technology.

Second, alliances between defense firms have become ever more important to the production and development of military technology. James Hasik notes in *Arms and Innovation* that many of the best-known military systems of the last decades have emerged from alliances between large, traditional defense producers and small, nontraditional firms.[6] These alliances inherently create the potential for conflicts over the ownership of technology and trade secrets, both between the firms themselves and between the firms and the government. To the extent that the nature of IP law affects the prospects of these alliances, it has an impact on military innovation.

Third, the importance of dual-use technologies, especially in the computing and communications sectors, has complicated the relationships that firms have with the government. While most firms like selling to the government, few nontraditional providers envision the Defense Department as their only customer. Rather, they plan to sell their technological innovations on the open market- hence, "dual use." State interest in acquiring the IP rights to the data, patents, and trade secrets of firms developing dual-use technologies runs directly counter to their commercial efforts.

Finally, private firms have, over the past five decades, committed an ever-increasing percentage of total funds devoted to technological research and development. At the same time, the government remains deeply involved in most defense research, committing substantial resources to the development of new weapon technologies. Most new systems, consequently, involve some mix of state and private funding. This creates problems for the ownership of the IP associated with technological innovations, problems that IP law can either solve or exacerbate.

While the broader project this article is associated with examines the role of IP law in both diffusion and innovation, this article concentrates on the former. Specifically, it examines how developments in IP law may have changed the nature of industrial espionage, especially in cyberspace. The article hopes to develop a framework for understanding the relevance of the efforts of the PLA to target the IP of defense-related firms in the United States and Europe.

---

[6] James M. Hasik, *Arms and Innovation: Entrepreneurship and Alliances in the Twenty-First-Century Defense Industry* (Chicago, IL: University of Chicago, 2008).

The Diffusion of Military Technology

The literature on diffusion in military affairs focuses on three questions. As characterized in the Davis and Eliason edited volume *The Diffusion of Military Technology and Doctrine*,

> "The first debate concerns how one defines the diffusion process, which is critical for identifying whether or not diffusion has occurred. The key question here is whether the communication of information is sufficient to conclude that diffusion has taken place... The second debate concerns the causes of diffusion. What motivates states to adopt innovations from abroad, and what is the mechanism by which knowledge is transferred? While scholars advance various typologies, three distinct processes— competition, socialization, and coercion—drive the spread of policies across societies with different implications for what is modeled. The third debate concerns the patterns and effects of diffusion."[7]

This study concentrates on the second of these three questions, the motivations and mechanisms of diffusion. Previous studies on why and how states seek to acquire technology have concentrated on material factors, organizational factors, and sociological factors. On the materialist pole, Joao Resende Santos argues the neorealist case for military diffusion. States adopt new doctrines, organizational modes, and technologies out of concern for their security, with adoption succeeding insofar as states can devote sufficient resources to the project.[8] In *The Diffusion of Military Power*, Michael C. Horowitz takes an organizational perspective to extend this case, arguing that differences between wealth and organizational complexity limit the diffusion of military power.[9]

Sociological explanations for institutions and behavior presuppose that humans live within a universe of social meanings. Although interest plays a role in behavior, appropriateness and legitimacy help construct the conditions under which states interpret interest. The behavior of others, especially powerful states, legitimates some behaviors and delegitimates others.[10] Norms and expectations structure how states pursue their interests.[11] Several scholars have applied this logic to procurement. Emily Goldman has explored how the impact of the Western military model differed in Japan

---

[7] Emily O. Goldman, and Leslie C. Eliason, *The Diffusion of Military Technology and Ideas* (Stanford, CA: Stanford University Press, 2003).

[8] JoãoResende-Santos, *Neorealism, States, and the Modern Mass Army* [Kindle Edition] (New York: Cambridge University Press, 2007).

[9] Michael Horowitz, *The Diffusion of Military Power: Causes and Consequences for International Politics* (Princeton, NJ: Princeton University Press, 2010).

[10] John W. Meyer, John Boli, George M. Thomas, and Francisco O. Ramirez, "World Society and the Nation State," *American Journal of Sociology* 103(1) (July 1997): 144–181, 146.

[11] Martha Finnemore, *The Purpose of Intervention: Changing Beliefs About the Use of Force* (Ithaca, NY: Cornell University Press, 2003), 16.

and Ottoman Turkey, and Theo Farrell has studied the effect of world military culture on the constitution of the Irish army.[12] Particularly relevant for this study, Dana Eyer and Mark Suchman established that poor countries buy expensive weapons, even when cheap weapons would better meet their needs.[13] Similarly, Daniel W. Henk and Marin R. Rupiya argue that symbolic logic drives much procurement strategy in African states.[14]

Mechanism: Industrial Espionage

This study seeks to meld sociological and materials logics of diffusion. The sociological framework allows that consequential and social logics interact, but specifying how, and under what conditions such interaction produced varied outcomes, is worth the effort. Ideas matter, and the presence of powerful ideational forces at the systemic level can cause states to redefine their identities and change the methods through which they pursue power.

In this study, we argue that a developing configuration of law and technology has made possible a new form of industrial espionage and that this form lies at the center of the struggle between China and the United States over the diffusion of military technology.

As mentioned in the introduction, one means of violating IP rights in the military sphere comes from the reverse engineering of technology acquired through legitimate or illegitimate means. As a practical matter, reverse engineering foreign technology for domestic production faces several difficult obstacles.[15] The thief needs to match, or come close to matching, the industrial and technological sophistication of the target. Taking apart an F-16 to figure out how it works is of no help if the thief cannot produce the components in question.

The appropriating state lacks trade secrets associated with the manufacturing of the system. At the very least, this can make the replication of foreign systems a costly and time-consuming process, as the appropriator needs to develop manufacturing procedures from scratch. At worst, it can lead to seriously substandard components that reduce the capabilities and reliability of a system. For example, Chinese efforts to

---

[12] Emily Goldman, "The Spread of Western Military Models to Ottoman Turkey and Meiji Japan," in *The Sources of Military Change: Culture, Politics, Technology, eds. Theo Farrell, and Terry Terriff* (Boulder, CO: Lynne Riener, 2002), 41–68, 43; Theo Farrell, "World Culture and the Irish Army, 1922–1942," in *The Sources of Military Change: Culture, Politics, Technology*, eds. Theo Farrell, and Terry Terriff, (Boulder, CO: Lynne Riener, 2002), 69–90, 82.

[13] Dana P. Eyer, and Mark C. Suchman, "Status, Norms, and the Proliferation of Conventional Weapons: An Institutional Theory Approach," in *The Culture of National Security*, ed. Peter J. Katzenstein (New York: Columbia University Press, 1996), 81.

[14] Daniel W. Henk, and Marin Revavi Rupiya, *Funding Defense: Challenges of Buying Military Capability in Sub-Saharan Africa* (Carlisle, PA: Strategic Studies Institute, 2001), 20.

[15] Stuart Macdonald, "Nothing Either Good or Bad: Industrial Espionage and Technology Transfer," *International Journal of Technology Management* 8 (1/2) (1993): 95.

reverse engineer certain Russian jet engines during the 1990s and 2000s invariably produced engines with extremely short lifespans and without the power of their Russian counterparts.[16]

Generally, the appropriator also lacks data associated with design and testing. Modern weapon systems generate an extraordinary amount of data during the development process, as computer models explore a vast array of scenarios with respect to potential components.[17] The testing process also generates data and the appropriating country generally lacks access to prototype models. The appropriating state generally lacks access to testing data associated with the system, which makes it difficult to come to solid conclusions regarding the tolerances of particular materials, or even the purpose of certain subcomponents.

Altogether, reverse engineering an entire system is generally more trouble than it is worth. States which have the industrial and technological capability to reverse engineer a complex system generally also have the capacity to engage in their own design work. Domestic designs mean that the builder can focus on weapon characteristics that it wants, rather than settle on a system designed by a foreign producer.

In some cases, however, reverse engineering makes sense. The difficulty of reverse engineering depends on the gap between industrial capabilities of the target and the appropriator and the amount of information that the appropriator has acquired. If the former is sufficiently small and the latter sufficiently large, an appropriator can profitably do the work necessary to copy a system or at least a group of subsystems.

In the case of cyber espionage, the evidence indicates that China's PLA has targeted exactly these kinds of systems. Instead of copying entire weapons, the Chinese have won access to data on the subsystems that give US weapons their lethality. These include "dual use" technologies that the United States has historical sought to prohibit from export. In addition to US government sources, Chinese hackers have targeted law firms, private corporations, foreign partners, and various intermediaries that possess access to data regarding dual use and military-only technologies.[18] Although the extent to which such data has found its way into Chinese systems remains uncertain, IP protection has become a central front in cyber conflict between the United States and China.

---

[16] Wendell Minnick, "Experts: China Still Lags West in Advanced Aircraft Technologies," *Defense News*, August 3, 2014, http://archive.defensenews.com/article/20140803/DEFREG03/308030011/Experts-China-Still-Lags-West-Advanced-Aircraft-Technologies.

[17] James Hasik, "Better Buying Power or Better Off Not? Purchasing Technical Data for Weapon Systems," *Defense Acquisition Research Journal* 21 (3) (July 2014): 697. See also Gilli, Andrea, and Mauro Gilli. "The Diffusion of Drone Warfare? Industrial, Organizational, and Infrastructural Constraints." *Security Studies* 25, no. 1 (2016): 50-84.

[18] James Vincent, "Schematics from Israel's Iron Dome Missile Shield 'Hacked' by Chinese, Says Report," *The Independent*, July 29, 2014.http://www.independent.co.uk/life-style/gadgets-and-tech/israels-iron-dome-missile-shield-hacked-by-chinese-military-hackers-says-report-9635619.html.

Cyber Conflict

Many studies have explored the founding of the internet, and the parallel growth of legitimate and illegitimate internet traffic.[19] Over the past decade, however, scholars and policymakers have increasingly concentrated on the prospects for and implication of "cyber conflict," which amounts to organized conflict between groups in cyberspace. This analysis has given good reason to suspect that cyber warfare differs from traditional warfare in consequential ways.

In *Cyber War versus Cyber Realities*, Brandon Valeriano and Ryan Maness define cyberspace as:

> the networked system of microprocessors, mainframes, and basic computers that act in digital space. Cyberspace has physical elements because these microprocessors, mainframes, and computers are systems with a physical location. Therefore, cyberspace is a physical, social-technological environment—a separate domain but one that interacts and blends with other domains and layers.[20]

They further define cyber conflict as:

> the use of computational technologies for malevolent and destructive purposes in order to impact, change, or modify diplomatic and military interactions between states.[21]

According to Valeriano and Maness, almost half of all cyber incidents involve theft, in which one state attempts to appropriate some kind of information from another.[22] In context of this paper, cyber conflict occurs when one state attempts to appropriate IP under the legal protection of another; this is to say, when a state or the agents of a state use access to digital space in order to steal legally defined property.

The concurrent development of cyberspace and the expansion of intellectual property law have changed the context in which states conduct industrial espionage.[23] The digitization of knowledge means that patent applications, trade secrets, and reams of industrial data have become available to talented hackers and dedicated organizations.

---

[19] See for example P.W. Singer, and Allan Friedman. *Cyber Security and Cyber War: What Everyone Needs to Know* (Oxford: Oxford University Press, 2014);Chris C. Demchak, Wars of Disruption and Resilience: Cybered Conflict, Power, and National Security(Athens: University of Georgia, 2011); Brandon Valeriano, and Ryan Maness, Cyber War versus Cyber Realities: Cyber Conflict in the International System (Oxford: Oxford University Press, 2015).

[20] Brandon Valeriano, and Ryan Maness. *Cyber War versus Cyber Realities: Cyber Conflict in the International System* (Oxford: Oxford University Press, 2015), 24.

[21] Ibid., 21.

[22] Ibid., 9.

[23] Carl Roper, *Trade Secret Theft, Industrial Espionage, and the China Threat.* Boca Raton: CRC Press, 2014, 197.

Moreover, the functioning of intellectual property law in the United States (and elsewhere) requires a degree of communication between different organizations. The military services, contractors, subcontractors, defense firms, and law firms all have some degree of access to crucial secrets.

In a sense, the vulnerability arises from changes in the nature of the defense industrial complex, and more broadly of modern capitalism. Specialization of firms increases inter-firm communications, which then creates communications vulnerabilities. Cooperation with the regulatory state complicates the picture even further. Many companies and legal firms have already begun to take steps to manage their vulnerability, including developing firewalls on communication with Chinese clients and affiliates. However, hackers have the luxury of concentrating on the weakest links.

Scholarship on the development of the information economy has long grappled with the shift from an industrial to a post-industrial, knowledge based economy.[24] Modern computing technology has enabled the collection of tremendous amounts of data, with processors allowing for search and analysis, and communications equipment facilitating near instantaneous transfer of information. Decades ago, the information contained in the databases mentioned above resided in huge warehouses, and could not effectively be "stolen" without immediate physical presence and the use of heavy equipment.

Cyber Security and the Public Private Bridge

Secretary of Defense Ash Carter elaborated on the Defense Department's view of cyber security clear in an April 2015 speech at Stanford University.[25] The location was not accidental, as the speech concentrated on the need for cooperation between the Pentagon and Silicon Valley. Carter argued that civilian innovation goes hand in hand with government action on cyber security. This relationship has four aspects:

(1) The increasing role that civilian investment plays in military technological innovation demands closer ties between the Department of Defense (DoD) and the centers of civilian innovation.
(2) Government investment and support have facilitated the development of many of the technologies central to digital innovation over the past several decades.

---

[24] Betz, David J., and Tim Stevens. "Chapter One: Power and cyberspace."*Adelphi Series* 51, no. 424 (2011): 35-54. See also Fritz Machlup, The Production and Distribution of Knowledge in the United States (Princeton, NJ: Princeton University Press, 1962); Peter F. Drucker, The Age of Discontinuity: Guidelines to Our Changing Society (1969; London: Pan Books, 1971); Daniel Bell, The Coming of the Post-Industrial Society: A Venture in Social Forecasting (London: Heinemann Educational, 1974); Christian Fuchs, Internet and Society: Social Theory in the Information Age (New York and Abingdon: Routledge, 2008).

[25] Ash Carter, "Rewiring the Pentagon: Charting a New Path on Innovation and Cyber Security," Department of Defense, April 23, 2015, http://www.defense.gov/Speeches/Speech.aspx?SpeechID=1935.

(3) Private firms and the government face different facets of the same cyber security problem, as espionage threats target both private and public sector entities.

(4) Private cyber security and publicly provided cyber security overlap; the defense of each depends on the security of the other, as both can come under attack, and vulnerabilities in one sector can lead to vulnerabilities in the other.

Yet some argue that the public–private partnership that interests Carter is particularly unlikely to develop in the tech sector.[26] Despite the critical role that government (and DoD) investment played in the foundation of the computing industry (and of the internet), technology firms and their workers tend not to share the values of the military–industrial complex or have much interest in securing government contracts. The Pentagon, operating under government employment restrictions, cannot compete with Silicon Valley salaries. Moreover, the revelations of Edward Snowden exacerbated a long-term political distrust between the government on one side, and left and libertarian leaning tech workers on the other.

The distrust between the Pentagon and Silicon Valley mirrors the problems that the DoD has faced in broadening its procurement base to civilian-oriented firms. In the case of cyber defense, however, the problem is even more serious; the DoD needs the active cooperation of technology and software firms in order to carry out its cyber security strategy. If private firms are vulnerable to espionage, then the DoD cannot defend its system of procurement or its basic military secrets. There is good reason to believe that hackers in the employ of the Chinese government have worked to exploit this seam.

US–China Cyber Conflict

Experts in the United States began to suspect in the mid-1990s that Chinese hackers were attempting secretly appropriate the technology—one may guess including trade secrets—of American firms working in critical strategic fields through a variety of cyber attacks. Recently, a report from the cyber security firm Mandiant argued that the PLA has played a central role in this process, with what amounts to the official sanction of Chinese government authorities.[27] According to Mandiant, a unit associated with the PLA has launched attacks against 141 global firms, many operating in the defense sector.[28] Although China is thought to the largest source

---

[26] Philip Ewing, "Ash Carter's appeal to Silicon Valley: We're 'Cool' Too." Politico, April 23, 2015, http://www.politico.com/story/2015/04/ash-carter-silicon-valley-appeal-117293.html.

[27] Center, Mandiant Intelligence. "APT1: Exposing one of China's cyber espionage units." *Mandian.com* (2013).

[28] Ibid., 3.

of attacks, Russia and India are also suspected of appropriating IP.[29] Reports indicate that these attacks have sought draft patent information, organizational strategy and hierarchy, and trade secrets.[30]

The data revealed by Edward Snowden and other sources indicates that the United States believes that China has appropriated a considerable amount of technology associated with numerous defense systems, including the F-35 Joint Strike Fighter, the General Atomics MQ-1 Predator drone, and others.[31] Classified presentation slides published by Der Spiegel indicate the loss of detailed information regarding radar design and engine schematics, as well as "terabytes" of engineering and testing data.[32] These slides also indicated a US government belief that it had suffered:[33]

- 30000 incidents
- 1600 computers penetrated
- 60000 user accounts compromised
- $100 to assess damage and repair networks
- 33000 USAF field officer records
- 30000 USN passwords
- Information on
    - Air refueling schedules
    - USTRASCOM (US Transportation Command) Single Mobility System
    - USN Missile and navigation systems
    - USN Nuclear submarine and anti-air missile designs
    - International Traffic and Arms Restrictions (ITAR data)
    - Data on B-2, F-22, F-35, and other systems

---

[29] Ellen Nakashima, "U.S. Launches Effort to Stem Trade Secret Theft," Washington Post, February 20, 2013, http://www.washingtonpost.com/world/national-security/us-launches-effort-to-stem-trade-secret-theft/2013/02/20/26b6fbce-7ba8-11e2-a044-676856536b40_story.html?hpid=z1; Devlin Barrett, "Many Past Espionage Cases Had Links to China," *Wall Street Journal*, February 20, 2013,http://online.wsj.com/article/SB10001424127887323864304578316612924601312.html.In just one of many examples, in September 2012, Sixing Liu was convicted in federal court in New Jersey for exporting U.S. military technology to China and stealing thousands of electronic files from his employer, L-3 Communications.

[30] Mandiant, 20.

[31] Bree Feng, "Among Snowden Leaks, Details of Chinese Cyberespionage," *New York Times*, January 20, 2015, http://sinosphere.blogs.nytimes.com/2015/01/20/among-snowden-leaks-details-of-chinese-cyberespionage/; Philip Dorling, "China Stole Plans for a New Fighter Plane, Spy Documents Have Revealed," Sydney Morning Herald, January 18, 2015 http://www.smh.com.au/national/china-stole-plans-for-a-new-fighter-plane-spy-documents-have-revealed-20150118-12sp1o.html

[32] National Security Agency, "Chinese Exfiltrate Sensitive Military Technology," *Der Spiegel*, http://www.spiegel.de/media/media-35687.pdf

[33] Ibid.

The US government has responded to concerns about cyber security by releasing a strategy for digital defense.[34] Initial steps include creating a watch list for regular cyber offenders and pressuring suspected countries in bilateral fora.[35] Critics of this approach have called for more robust steps, including support for lawsuits, prosecutions, and visa denials of officials from suspected countries and firms.[36] At the same time, planners have debated the strategic implications of cyber conflict.[37] The participation of an active duty PLA unit in efforts to steal US defense sector-related IP indicates that state behavior (in the field of espionage and counterespionage) is adapting to new technological and legal realities. The strategic relevance of cybercrime becomes tied to the rise of IP as a critical national concern.

In May 2014, the US Department of Justice indicted five officers of the PLA on charges of cyber theft.[38] The US indictment established an important distinction between US espionage policy and Chinese policy. The key difference, according to US policymakers, is that the PLA hackers stole information from private US firms and turned that information over to Chinese state owned firms. US espionage, on the other hand, concentrates on governments and state-owned firms. While the information gained from such espionage may benefit private American firms, it does not involve the straightforward transfer of foreign information to privately owned American companies.

This makes the theft of private, national security-related IP very interesting in context of the development of the modern national innovation system. Virtually every patent owned by traditional national security providers in the United States involves de facto collaboration between the US government and a private actor. Moreover, the steadily expanding involvement of private firms in the defense sector in the United States (and elsewhere) means that cyber attacks on private firms can amount to defense-oriented industrial espionage.

Concerns about the F-35 loom particularly large. The DoD expects the F-35, a product of Lockheed Martin, to fill out the fighter-bomber fleets of not only the US Air Force, US Marine Corps, and US Navy, but also the fleets of nearly a dozen allied states. China could use technical information appropriated from the F-35 project in several ways. First, it could apply technical know-how to efforts to detect and defeat the F-35. This would involve improving the capabilities of Chinese detection and weapons systems in ways that could ensure detection and a successful kill following detection. Potentially, China could share this information with other interested states, just as the United States,

---

[34] White House, *Administration Strategy on Mitigating the Theft of U.S. Trade Secrets* (Washington, DC: United States Government, 2013).

[35] Nakashima, "U.S. Launches Effort to Stem Trade Secret Theft."

[36] Ibid.

[37] W. Alexander Vacca, "Military Culture and Cyber Security," *Survival: Global Politics and Strategy* 53 (6), December 2011–January 2012):159–176.

[38] Department of Justice, "U.S. Charges Five Chinese Military Hackers for Cyber Espionage against U.S. Corporations and a Labor Organization for Commercial Advantage," May 19, 2014 http://www.justice.gov/opa/pr/us-charges-five-chinese-military-hackers-cyber-espionage-against-us-corporations-and-labor.

Israel, and others shared information about Soviet MiGs with one another during the Cold War.[39] This would fall into a traditional understanding of military espionage and would not represent a significant violation of the IP rights of US firms.

Alternatively, China could use the appropriated technical information to improve its own jet fighters, potentially competing with US aircraft. Some indications suggest that China is moving in precisely this direction. The J-31 fighter prototype, produced by the Chinese military aviation firm Shenyang, reportedly has many features that Shenyang has directly copied from the F-35.[40] The two aircraft are not identical; the J-31 has two engines to the F-35s one, and the J-31 lacks the architecture for VSTOL flight that is central to the F-35. Nevertheless, some similarities suggest that Shenyang had access to proprietary information about the F-35 when designing the J-31.

Adding to the complication, recent reports have indicated that China plans the export of the J-31, and indeed that Shenyang may build the aircraft primarily for the export, rather than the domestic, market.[41] This would put the J-31 into direct competition with the F-35, as the only fifth-generation stealth fighters currently available (the Russian PAK-FA may soon be available to limited customers). Potentially, this could open Shenyang (and the Chinese government) up to legal action under several instruments of international IP law. While it is unlikely that the United States (or any international organization) could enforce a settlement inside China, a ruling could potentially affect Shenyang's assets abroad.

To be sure, the United States and other countries also engage in cyber espionage, although this espionage generally has different implications for IP law. Reportedly, the US intelligence community (IC) has historically supplied US firms with a variety of intelligence designed to improve their market position and negotiation strategies.[42] The IC has also fed intelligence about foreign military equipment into the private sector of the defense industrial base, although it is less clear that this intelligence gathering has directly affected the ability of US firms to compete with foreign products.[43]

---

[39] Steve Davies, *Red Eagles: America's Secret MiGs* (Oxford: Osprey Pub., 2008).

[40] Dave Majumdar, "U.S. Pilots Say New Chinese Stealth Fighter Could Become Equal of F-22, F-35," United States Naval Institute, November 5, 2014 http://news.usni.org/2014/11/05/u-s-pilots-say-new-chinese-stealth-fighter-become-equal-f-22-f-35.

[41] Robert Farley, "China's Selling the J-31, But Who's Buying?" Diplomat APAC, November 14, 2014. http://thediplomat.com/2014/11/chinas-selling-the-j-31-but-whos-buying/.

[42] David Sanger, and Tim Weiner, "Emerging Role for the C.I.A.: Economic Spy," *New York Times*, October 15, 1995, http://www.nytimes.com/1995/10/15/world/emerging-role-for-the-cia-economic-spy.html.

[43] Ibid.

Industrial Espionage and the Chinese MIC

History of the Chinese MIC

An explanation of how Chinese cyber espionage affects the diffusion of military technology to China, as well as the innovation process within China, can benefit from a discussion of the history and nature of the military-industrial complex of the PRC. In 1949, the Chinese defense industry produced little in the way of sophisticated military technology. World War II and the Chinese Civil War had destroyed much of the urban industrial base, and the Soviets had confiscated much of the industrial equipment the Japanese had brought to Manchuria. The dire economic situation that faced the PRC in the wake of the revolution made for minimal investment in technological development.

As initially established, the Chinese military–industrial complex distinguished between the strategic weapons complex (nuclear weapons and their delivery systems) and the conventional weapons complex.[44] The former would have the latitude to engage in basic research, as well as a degree of protection from the vagaries of Chinese Communist Party (CCP) politics. The latter would concentrate on production, imitation of foreign technology, and incremental improvement. The strategic complex managed to develop nuclear weapons with minimal foreign assistance in conditions of tremendous poverty. The conventional weapons complex produced a huge number of obsolescent planes, tanks, and ships, often a generation behind the industry standard. Both sides relied on state investment in large-scale, state-owned enterprises.

In the late 1990s and 2000s, the CCP pushed a major set of reforms through the defense industry.[45] The largest, most important firms remained state owned, but were forced to reform in order to increase efficiency and responsiveness, and reduce cost. The government tried to create a competitive environment by splitting firms and setting them against one another, and by stepping up purchases from Russia. Reforms to the system of IP law helped incentivize information sharing and an across-the-board regulatory effort helped bring many firms up to international standards.

The innovative capacity of an MIC extends to more than just the military and the defense industry.[46] It also involves the constellation of labs, research facilities, and universities that facilitate innovation in both the civilian and military economies. This system has existed in some form since the Maoist period, but reforms have attempted to make it more competitive, and more receptive to foreign technology (and even foreign capital). These reforms have helped make the current Chinese defense sector more healthy and innovative than ever. Indeed, unlike the MICs of the United States and Europe, the Chinese defense sector has enjoyed consistent increases in procurement funding.

---

[44] Tai Ming Cheung, *Fortifying China: The Struggle to Build a Modern Defense Economy* [Kindle] (Ithaca: Cornell University Press, 2013), 992.

[45] Cheung, 1421.

[46] Cheung, 390.

This is not to say that the Chinese defense sector is competitive with the most innovative firms in Europe, Japan, and the United States. Most sectors of the defense industry have concentrated on incremental innovations, adapting newly developed and acquired technologies to old platforms in small batch construction. China has most effectively specialized in what scholars describe as "architectural" innovation;[47] innovations that shifts and repurposes existing technologies in new forms, hopefully with emergent qualities. Architectural innovations can reap tremendous rewards in military technology; the world-beating battleship HMS Dreadnought, for example, represented an architectural innovation. Similarly, the Df-21 carrier-killer anti-ship ballistic missile repurposes existing technology in more deadly form.

China has long exported military equipment to the world, but for most of the post-war period this has involved second-rate, low-technology weapons. The increasing sophistication of the Chinese MIC could make it more competitive for higher tech equipment, but China has had trouble breaking into some of the more lucrative markets. China may be on the verge of some success with the JF-17 fighter, although as this aircraft strongly resembles an updated MiG-21, it does not serve to demonstrate cutting edge technological innovation. Thus far the only customer is Pakistan, but rumors suggest that Nigeria, Egypt, and Argentina may all have some interest.

Public-Private

Historically, China's defense-industrial base (like its Soviet model) relied on large, state-owned industry to shoulder the burden of innovation and production. The Soviet industrial system tends to support incremental innovation, but struggles to develop new, novel technology. Both the Chinese and the Soviets before them have relied on injections of foreign technology, either through espionage or purchase, to invigorate their defense industries.

The reforms of the 1980s and 1990s pushed the defense industry into the civilian economy, often unwillingly.[48] Firms often had to restructure in order to produce goods for the civilian market, which sometimes reduced efficiency and innovative capacity. However, this restructuring also tended to improve the internal operation of firms, familiarizing them with the prospects of the civilian market.

More recently, the Chinese defense industry has moved toward the Western model, with strong ties developing between large, state-owned defense enterprises and smaller technology firms. In the Chinese case, the lack of access of traditional defense providers to the wider world of military technology (a leftover from 1990s era sanctions resulting from the Tiananmen Square massacre) make it even more important for Chinese defense firms to work with their civilian counterparts.[49]

---

[47] Samm Tyroler-Cooper, and Alison Peet, "The Chinese Aviation Industry: Techno-Hybrid Patterns of Development in the C919 Program," in *China's Emergence as a Defense Technological Power* [Kindle], ed. Tai Ming Cheung (London: Routledge, 2013), 2423.
[48] Cheung, 1496, 2000.
[49] Ibid., 2147.

Industrial Espionage

How much does the Chinese MIC depend on foreign technology? Opinions differ, but most analysts say "a lot." Just on the aerospace side, the influence of foreign technology is clear. The J-10 was based on the IAI Lavi and the General Dynamics F-16; the J-11 is a clone of the Su-27; the JF-17 is a modern development of the MiG-21; and finally, the J-31 is widely reputed to rely heavily on technology associated with the Lockheed Martin F-35.[50]

China acquires foreign technology through various means, both above and below board.[51] On the private side, Chinese firms operating abroad, and in partnership with foreign firms domestically, have access to an array of foreign technologies and production methods. Chinese students study in Europe, Australia, and the United States, becoming familiar with techniques developed in the world's most advanced research universities. China also acquires weapons and technology transfers through legitimate purchase.

However, we do not yet have a sense of how stolen IP finds its way into the Chinese MIC. Industrial espionage sounds intriguing, but there are many practical obstacles to the successful theft of technology.[52] Individual bits of data, even sophisticated data associated with patents and trade secrets, mean little out of context. Would-be thieves need to know a lot about their target, as well as a great deal about the subject matter involved.

In order to produce useful innovation, the cyber soldiers of the PLA need to know where to direct their efforts, and what they need to look for.[53] This requires close collaboration between the MIC (which knows what it needs) and the cyber teams (which know where to look). We don't know how responsive the PLA is to requests for information from the MIC, or from private industry. We also don't know how stolen information finds its way into the MIC, either on the public or the private side.

Thus far, we have considerable evidence that the PLA steals military-oriented technology from the United States and Europe, and some evidence that it has successfully put this technology to use. During a recent military parade marking the 70th anniversary of the defeat of Japan, the Voice of America listed the foreign-sourced equipment participating in the demonstration, including the HQ-6A surface-to-air missile battery (appropriated from Italy), the J-15 carrier-based fighter, and several other pieces of equipment.[54] In most cases, however, the fruits of espionage come in subsystems, rather than in complete weapons.

---

[50] Carlo Kopp, "Chengdu J-10: Technical Report APA-TR-2007-0701," Air Power Australia, January 27, 2014. http://www.ausairpower.net/APA-Sinocanard.html.

[51] William C. Hannas, James Mulvenon, and Anna B. Puglisi, *Chinese Industrial Espionage: Technology Acquisition and Military Modernization* [Kindle] (London: Routledge, 2013).

[52] Macdonald, Stuart. "Nothing either good or bad: Industrial espionage and technology transfer." *International Journal of Technology Management* 8.1-2 (1993): 95-105.

[53] Roper, 103.

[54] Salgal Dasgupta, "Analysts: Beijing Parade a 'Bazaar' of Stolen Technology," *Voice of America*, September 4, 2015. http://www.voanews.com/content/analysts-beijing-military-parade-a-bazaar-of-stolen-technology/2946768.html.

Most of the successful Chinese projects have required either significant production data (as was the case with the J-10) or the acquisition of export models (the Su-27). As Chinese products have grown in sophistication, they have begun to compete with targeted systems. The most obvious competition has come from efforts to export the J-11 Flanker clone, but China's air defense systems have also sparked some interest around the world. The export of stolen technology, however, would open Chinese firms up to an array of potential legal challenges from Russian and Western firms.

China suffers from an additional problem, as its defense industries remain cut off from much of the global arms market. This limits the access of Chinese defense firms to the latest products, technologies, and manufacturing systems. Chinese firms still have some access to the Russian defense industry, but Russia has limited access after a series of controversies over stolen technology, and in any case the Chinese have learned most of what they can from the Russians.

Conclusions

The expansion of IP law, as with many technological and legal developments, has the potential to create contradictory effects on international espionage. On the one hand, the accumulation of data, ease of cyber access, and proliferation of actors makes it easier for hackers and spies to acquire IP. On the other hand, the growing acceptance of international IP law may offer victims a new set of instruments for fighting espionage.

As Susan Sell has argued, international IP protection is, in and of itself, a power play on the part of major economic actors.[55] The construction and maintenance of the rule systems owes itself to the entrepreneurial behavior of private business, working not only through the US government, but also through international institutions. As such, power relations are embedded within the rules of the IP system, and within our entire way of talking about IP. This is one reason why the IP provisions of the Trans–Pacific Partnership have proven so controversial.

But adherence to international institutional frameworks isn't entirely voluntary. The demands of international organizations (and, in bilateral terms, of the EU and the United States) require the Chinese government to develop a position on IP, a set of policies designed to support that position, and the bureaucracy necessary to execute those policies.[56] While this bureaucracy may lack power initially, over time the state acquires what amount to habits of compliance, where it becomes more problematic to step outside the expectations of the international regime than to stay within them. In *China Goes Global*, David Shambaugh outlines this process with respect to China's engagement with the various regimes of the liberal international economic order.

[55] Sell, 80.
[56] Ministry of Commerce, "Intellectual Property Protection in China," http://www.chinaipr.gov.cn/.

Thus, the development of a bureaucracy to manage IP rights, which China has begun, almost inevitably produces a policy shift toward compliance.[57] To the extent that the IP regime (in its several institutional faces, including Trade-Related Intellectual Property Rights (TRIPS), the World Trade Organization (WTO), and others) helps form guidelines for appropriate national behavior, the PRC may rein in or otherwise modify the behavior of its military intelligence apparatus.

In any case, a full analysis of the implications of cyber warfare for industrial espionage requires considerably more research. This article hopes to lay the foundation for that research. The future of the Chinese MIC depends, to some extent, on its ability to acquire technology from the United States and elsewhere. The future of US–Chinese relations depends, to some extent, on the size and sophistication of the Chinese MIC.

References

Betz, David J. and Tim Stevens. 2011. "Chapter One: Power and cyberspace." *Adelphi Series* 51 (424).

Center, Mandiant Intelligence. 2013. "APT1: Exposing one of China's cyber espionage units." *Mandiant. com.*

Cheung, Tai Ming. 2013. *Fortifying China: The Struggle to Build a Modern Defense Economy* (Ithaca: Cornell University Press).

Davies, Steve. 2008. *Red Eagles: America's Secret MiGs* (Oxford: Osprey).

Eyer, Dana P. and Mark C. Suchman. 1996. "Status, Norms, and the Proliferation of Conventional Weapons: An Institutional Theory Approach," in *The Culture of National Security*, ed. Peter J. Katzenstein (New York: Columbia University Press).

Farrell, Theo Farrell. 2002. "World Culture and the Irish Army, 1922–1942," in *The Sources of Military Change: Culture, Politics, Technology*, eds. Theo Farrell, and Terry Terriff, (Boulder, CO: Lynne Riener).

Gilli, Andrea and Mauro Gilli. 2016. "The Diffusion of Drone Warfare? Industrial, Organizational, and Infrastructural Constraints." *Security Studies* 25 (1).

---

[57] David Shambaugh, *China Goes Global: The Partial Power* (Oxford: Oxford University Press, 2013), 131.

Goldman, Emily. 2002. "The Spread of Western Military Models to Ottoman Turkey and Meiji Japan," in *The Sources of Military Change: Culture, Politics, Technology*, eds. Theo Farrell, and Terry Terriff (Boulder, CO: Lynne Riener).

Goldman, Emily O. and Leslie C. Eliason. 2003. *The Diffusion of Military Technology and Ideas* (Stanford, CA: Stanford University Press).

Hasik, James M. 2008. *Arms and Innovation: Entrepreneurship and Alliances in the Twenty-First-Century Defense Industry* (Chicago, IL: University of Chicago).

Hasik, James. 2014. "Better Buying Power or Better Off Not? Purchasing Technical Data for Weapon Systems," *Defense Acquisition Research Journal* 21 (3).

Hannas, William C., James Mulvenon, and Anna B. Puglisi. 2013. *Chinese Industrial Espionage: Technology Acquisition and Military Modernization* (London: Routledge).

Henk, Daniel W., and Marin Revavi Rupiya. 2001. *Funding Defense: Challenges of Buying Military Capability in Sub-Saharan Africa* (Carlisle, PA: Strategic Studies Institute).

Finnemore, Martha. 2003. *The Purpose of Intervention: Changing Beliefs About the Use of Force* (Ithaca, NY: Cornell University Press).

Horowitz, Michael. 2010. *The Diffusion of Military Power: Causes and Consequences for International Politics* (Princeton, NJ: Princeton University Press).

Macdonald, Stuart. 1993. "Nothing Either Good or Bad: Industrial Espionage and Technology Transfer," *International Journal of Technology Management* 8 (1/2).

Paarlberg, Robert L. 2004. "Knowledge as Power: Science, Military Dominance, and U.S. Security," *International Security* 29 (1).

Resende-Santos, João. 2007. *Neorealism, States, and the Modern Mass Army* (New York: Cambridge University Press).

Meyer, John W., John Boli, George M. Thomas, and Francisco O. Ramirez. 1997. "World Society and the Nation State," *American Journal of Sociology* 103 (1).

Roper, Carl. 2014. *Trade Secret Theft, Industrial Espionage, and the China Threat.* (Boca Raton: CRC Press).

Sell, Susan K. 2003. *Private Power, Public Law: The Globalization of Intellectual Property Rights* (Cambridge: Cambridge University Press).

Singer, P.W. and Allan Friedman. 2014. *Cyber Security and Cyber War: What Everyone Needs to Know* (Oxford: Oxford University Press).

Shambaugh, David. 2013. *China Goes Global: The Partial Power* (Oxford: Oxford University Press).

Tyroler-Cooper, Samm and Alison Peet. 2013. "The Chinese Aviation Industry: Techno-Hybrid Patterns of Development in the C919 Program," in *China's Emergence as a Defense Technological Power,* ed. Tai Ming Cheung (London: Routledge).

Vacca, W. Alexander. 2012. "Military Culture and Cyber Security," *Survival: Global Politics and Strategy* 53 (6).

Valeriano, Brandon and Ryan Maness. 2015. *Cyber War versus Cyber Realities: Cyber Conflict in the International System* (Oxford: Oxford University Press).

White House. 2013. *Administration Strategy on Mitigating the Theft of U.S. Trade Secrets* (Washington, DC: United States Government).

Reacting to Cyber Threats: Protection and Security in the Digital Age

Anthony Craig [A] & Brandon Valeriano[B]

The cyber threat is now a major source of concern in contemporary security affairs and for many governments worldwide cyberspace now represents a new warfighting domain. Given these heightened levels of fear, it is important to ask what steps are being taken by states in response to the threat. A worrying development is the supposed cyber arms race in offensive capabilities given the propensity of these processes to escalate already high levels of tensions between rivals. At the same time, there are suggestions that proper defensive measures have not being given the utmost priority that they arguably should be. Despite speculation, these questions have not been subjected to empirical and data-driven analysis. This article investigates the reaction to the cyber threat by first examining the relationship between threat perception and the presence of offensive capabilities, and then engages the question of whether states are improving their nationwide defensive infrastructure in response to fear. Our results suggest that the heightened perception of threat is indeed linked to the possession of offensive capabilities, but we find little evidence to show that the cyber fear is motivating states to improve their basic cyber hygiene through the use of encrypted server technologies.

Key words: *cyber security, threat, offense, defense*

Introduction

In this highly interconnected digital era, cyber threats now represent one of the most urgent national security concerns. This has prompted governments worldwide to reconfigure their military strategies to prepare for battle in cyberspace, now considered a domain of warfare alongside land, sea, air, and space.[1] Cyber has become a particularly critical issue within US political discourse with the Director of National Intelligence James Clapper consistently naming it as the top security concern over the past few years.[2] This heightened level of fear is also reflected in American society at large

---

[A] Cardiff University

[B] Cardiff University and Donald Bren Chair of Armed Conflict, Marine Corps University

[1] *"War in the fifth domain,"* The Economist, July 1, 2010, http://www.economist.com/node/16478792

[2] G. Taylor, *"James Clapper, Intel Chief: Cyber Ranks Highest on Worldwide Threats to U.S.,"* Washington Times, Feb 26, 2015, http://www.washingtontimes.com/news/2015/feb/26/james-clapper-intel-chief-cyber-ranks-highest-worl/?page=all

doi: 10.18278/gsis.1.2.3

as is evident in a 2015 global threat survey which found that 59% of the US public felt "very concerned" about the "risk of cyber attacks on governments, banks, or corporations".[3] The cyber threat is ranked up there with and often supersedes other pressing security threats like ISIS, a rising China, or a resurgent Russia, as commentators warn of a "Cyber Pearl Harbor" suggesting a devastating cyber incident against the state's critical infrastructure is inevitable.[4] Fear clearly runs high in the cyber domain and a key question to address is what kind of reaction these heightened levels of threat perception are provoking.

An ongoing debate within the cyber security field centers on the issue of whether this level of perceived threat is justified, and if the prospect of cyber conflict represents a revolution in how states should think about their national security, or whether the risk is instead largely exaggerated by the military bureaucracies, security firms, and the media outlets who often stand to gain from threat inflation. Empirical studies suggest that the threat is hyped to a large extent (Lindsay 2013; Valeriano and Maness 2015), yet the critical query skipped thus far in the debate regards the nature of the reaction. It is important to pay close attention to how states react to their perceived fears because we should be concerned with encouraging policy responses that are proportional to the reality of the dangers in the international system and effective in increasing security.

One way in which states can react to the threat is through offensive cyber technologies that are wielded as an assumed deterrent against potential aggressors in cyberspace. Many countries appear to be seeking to enhance their cyber warfare capabilities by establishing cyber command units and hiring teams of professional hackers, and these actions may be symptomatic of what is increasingly being referred to as the "cyber" arms race (Craig and Valeriano 2016; Diebert 2011). While it is urgent we pay attention to these offensive developments, we should also ask how states are responding in terms of their defensive and protective infrastructure. This is arguably the sensible first step governments should take in response to their security fears, in contrast to the build-up of offensive capabilities which risks setting off security dilemmas and escalating levels of tension and conflict.

Our research question is particularly critical in light of suggestions that proper defensive measures are not being given priority (Rid 2013). The US Department of Homeland Security for example is charged with protecting the nation-state against incoming attacks, yet an internal audit reported numerous fatal flaws in security systems as well as a lack of training among cyber security professionals.[5] The hack of the Office of Personnel Management (OPM) in June 2015 resulted in 22.5 million sensitive records being stolen, but this breach did not occur due to the skill of the attacker but rather

---

[3] J. Carle, *"Climate Change Seen as Top Global Threat,"* Pew Research Center, July 14, 2015, http://www. pewglobal.org/files/2015/07/Pew-Research-Center-Global-Threats-Report-FINAL-July-14-2015.pdf

[4] While these threats may overlap, public opinion surveys ask the question in such a way as to make these threats different.

[5] A. Carman, *"DHS Websites Vulnerable to Exploits Amid Lacking Cyber Security Training,"* SC Magazine, September 17, 2015, http://www.scmagazine.com/oig-issues-department-of-homeland-security-report/article/439025/?utm_content=bufferc11a1&utm_medium=social&utm_source=twitter.com&utm_campaign=buffer

the incompetence of the systems administrators and the connections with external contractors.[6] Rather than upgrade their systems to prepare for the increasing online threats, the US Navy even continues to pay Microsoft to support the outdated and vulnerable Windows XP platform.[7] And despite the Department of Homeland Security's attempts to secure government networks through the deployment of the EINSTEIN intrusion detection system, it has been reported that these systems fail to detect 94% of the most common types of vulnerabilities.[8] These examples suggest that there is room for improvement in the state's basic cyber hygiene practices that should be given at least as much, if not more, consideration than offensive cyber posturing.

This article investigates reactions to the cyber threat and particular attention is paid to whether states are responding by improving their cyber security infrastructure. In doing so this article continues the rise of the social science perspective in this new area of security studies by using data and evidence to engage critical cyber security questions. While examples and case studies can be illustrative and illuminating, they fail to provide us with a macro picture of state behavior in the international cyber domain. One can tell a harrowing story of the Stuxnet cyber attack and its impacts as if it was a James Bond story rewritten for modern times, but these illustrations have little connection to the general trends in the field. Our approach is to provide a statistical analysis of the issue using the available data to uncover global patterns in cyber security practices in the international system.

Cyber Threats and Their Reactions

Concerns over politically motivated, destructive attacks from other states or terrorists groups are what motivated the "cyber Pearl Harbor" warning by the then US Defense Secretary Leon Panetta in 2012. This type of threat can be described as sabotage or cyber conflict defined as "the use of computational technologies in cyberspace for malevolent and/or destructive purposes in order to impact, change, or modify diplomatic and military interactions between entities" (Valeriano and Maness 2015). These types of actions can be launched against a nation's critical infrastructure, much of which is connected to and operated by internet networks. Such an attack, in theory, has the potential to shut down electricity grids or financial systems and create chaos within society, although an incident on such a destructive scale has yet to take place. In these attacks, there is clear coercive intent.

---

[6] A. Elkus, "*No Patch For Incompetence,*" War on the Rocks, June 23, 2015, http://warontherocks. com/2015/06/no-patch-for-incompetence-our-cybersecurity-problem-has-nothing-to-do-with-cybersecurity/

[7] R. Hackett, "*Why the U.S. Navy is Still Paying Microsoft Millions for Windows XP,*" Fortune, June 24, 2015, http://fortune.com/2015/06/24/navy-microsoft-windows-xp/

[8] A. Sternstein, "*US Homeland Security's $6B Firewall Has More Than a Few Frightening Blind Spots,*" Defense One, January 29, 2016, http://www.defenseone.com/technology/2016/01/us-homeland-securitys-6b-firewall-has-more-few-frightening-blind-spots/125528/?oref=DefenseOneFB

Much more widespread is the activity of cyber espionage, or the "attempt to penetrate an adversarial computer network or system for the purpose of extracting sensitive or protected information" (Rid 2013). Cyber espionage is a form of computer network attack (CNA) that can also come in the form of coercive attempts and disruption events (Jensen, Maness, and Valeriano. 2016). The 2009 theft of the F-35 fighter designs from the US military by Chinese hackers is one of the most high-profile cases of cyber espionage. Cybercrime is another threat that applies to society more generally. It involves the financially motivated theft of information and tends to be carried out by non-state actors or individuals lacking political motivations.

Scholars working on these issues are split on the level of risk they represent. Some see the rapid technological change in the information age as causing the greatest revolution in military affairs of our time (Clarke and Knake 2010; Kello 2013). This is known as the cyber revolution hypothesis, whose proponents argue that the unique characteristics of the cyber domain, such as the lack of geographical constraints, the problem of attribution, the involvement of non-state actors, and the low cost of offensive cyber tools in relation to defense, make the cyber threat difficult to counter and thus represents a new and serious risk to the security of the nation-state. Others are more moderate about the reality of the danger facing us and argue against the overhyping of threat. Rid (2013) for one rejects the use of the term cyber warfare, raising the point that it has yet to result in a single casualty. In an analysis of the 2011 Stuxnet attack against Iran's nuclear program, Lindsay (2013) shows that such a sophisticated computer virus costs hundreds of millions of dollars to develop and could only have been created by a technological superpower like the United States. Providing a broad picture of the cyber threat landscape, Valeriano and Maness (2015) collect data on cyber incidents between rival states and find that only 16% have engaged in cyber conflict and the incidents that do occur generally exhibit low levels of severity.

Yet regardless of the actual danger cyber conflict represents, the perception of threat is undoubtedly very high. International Relations scholarship has long emphasized the role perceptions play in shaping the state's reaction to threat through the process of the security dilemma (Jervis 1978). A state's decision to build-up armaments is often based, as Hammond (1993) notes, "on the subjective interpretations of the actions of others" rather than on accurate information and real events. The role that psychology plays is especially important to factor into the study of the cyber domain given the fact that we have yet to witness a catastrophic computer network attack. The threats are clearly constructed as much by perceptions as by reality, and these perceptions alone are able to dramatically alter the strategic landscape (Dunn Cavelty 2012). We can therefore expect perceptions of threat to impact national security policies and the development of a state's cyber capabilities.

This research taps into the broader issue regarding the appropriate type of response to cyber security threats. The hack of the OPM in 2014, widely believed to have been carried out by China, has added fuel to the debate over how exactly the United States should respond to such acts of cyber aggression. The White House did not publicly blame China for the attack and the American response has been restrained as it seeks to avoid escalation, but at the Aspen Security Forum Senator John McCain criticized the lack of reaction and clear policy.[9] The question is whether the focus ought to be on prevention and defense or, as McCain himself advocates, hacks like that of the OPM should be considered an act of war, best met with retaliation to allow the United States to demonstrate its superior capabilities and resolve in dissuading further intrusions into its networks. There have been many calls for a firmer policy of deterrence in cyberspace, yet much less has been said about what the government can do to bolster its own defenses and to reinforce greater cyber hygiene nationwide.

The distinction between offense and defense is regularly made when discussing cyber capabilities, and much attention has been paid to the notion that the cyber domain favors the former. Offensive cyber weaponry is considered more cost effective with one military official claiming that it costs 10 times as much to defend against malware as it does to mount an offensive operation (Fahrenkrug 2012). Defensive measures on the other hand are considered to be less efficient because of the immense challenge involved in securing every civilian and privately owned network and to close every vulnerability, many of which go undetected until an attack has pointed them out (Liff 2012).

If the domain is indeed offense oriented, it raises a challenge for the future of international security. In the traditional International Relations discourse, offense–defense balance theory predicts that if offensive military capabilities hold an advantage over defensive capabilities, the security dilemma is more intense and the risk of arms races and war greater (Glaser and Kaufmann 1998). Although there is little statistical evidence that either the perceived or actual offense–defense balance in the international system predicts militarized disputes and war (Gortzak, Haftel, and Sweeney 2005), its impact on interstate competition and arms races may nevertheless be substantial. If this is true of the cyber domain, we may unfortunately witness a greater development of offensive capabilities at the expensive of the defense, and an escalation of fear and tension within the international system. There are already signs that this proposition is becoming a reality with several media sources making claims of a "cyber" arms race[10]. Moreover, research by the United Nations Institute for Disarmament Research finds that 47 countries worldwide have begun to integrate cyber warfare units, strategies, and doctrines into their military organizational structures.[11]

The rationale behind the development of offensive capabilities as a national security policy is to send a clear message to potential aggressors of one's willingness and capacity to retaliate in the hope of deterring attacks in the first place (Huth and Russett 1990). Analysts often use this framework of deterrence theory in discussions about the use of cyber weaponry, forgetting however that the secrecy states keep over their cyber capabilities makes deterrence a problematic strategy if the goal is to make clear

---

[9] D. Verton, *"U.S. Cyber Policy Struggles to Keep up with Events,"* Fedscoop, July 27, 2015, http://fedscoop. com/u-s-cyber-policy-struggling-to-keep-up-with-events

[10] G. Corera, *"Rapid Escalation of the Cyber-Arms Race,"* BBC News, April 29, 2015, http://www.bbc. co.uk/news/uk-32493516

[11] UNIDIR, *"The Cyber Index: International Security Trends and Realities,"* March 2013, http://www. unidir.org/files/publications/pdfs/cyber-index-2013-en-463.pdf

one's capacity to retaliate (Valeriano and Maness 2016). Furthermore, the large body of International Relations research demonstrating a link between military build-ups and the escalation of disputes (Gibler, Rider, and Hutchison 2005; Sample 1997; Vasquez 1993; Wallace 1979) suggests that confrontational policies in cyberspace will only serve to intensify cyber conflict.

There are other paths forward in improving state security, and if the fault of the Sony hack, the OPM hack, and countless other violations lies with those who run the security apparatus within states and private companies, might the first task rationally be to prepare the defenses and establish a resilient cyber industry that meets future challenges? There is a clear need in the cyber domain, no matter what perspective one has of the threat, to bolster defensive and resiliency strategies.

The benefit of cyber defensive measures, such as through the encryption of data or improved methods of threat sharing and detection, is that they cannot be seen as threatening weapons to other states, unlike the creation of explicitly attack oriented cyber warfare units. Developing offensive weapons is sure to activate the traditional security dilemma suggesting that defensive measures instead should be encouraged. The cyber security field has not adequately investigated the nature of cyber defenses in the macro-political context. The central aim of this article is to examine how states are reacting to the cyber threat both offensively and, but more importantly, in terms of defensive cyber infrastructure improvements by using the specific indicator of encrypted web servers.

Research Design

Our data analysis includes a number of techniques ranging from identifying simple bivariate associations to multivariate regression modeling. Cyber threats represent our explanatory variable in this analysis, and our aim is to measure the reaction to such fears. To gauge the level of cyber threat experienced by states we use survey data from the 2015 Pew Research Center study which asks the public their views on a range of global security issues. Alongside the other contemporary issues of climate change, economic instability, the terrorist threat from ISIS, the risk of Iran acquiring nuclear weapons, as well as the tensions regarding Russia and China and their neighbors, a sample of respondents in each of 39 countries worldwide were asked about their level of concern about the risks of "cyber attacks on government, banks, or corporations."[12] We create our threat perception variable by combining the percentage responses of those "very concerned" with those "somewhat concerned" about the cyber threat. This gauges the level of priority given to cyber threats in the population's national security concerns. The survey covers a geographically and economically varied range of countries, with the threat perception ranging from a low of 18% (Ukraine) to a high of 88% (South Korea), with a mean of 60%. Later on in our investigation, we utilize data on actual cyber incidents which allows us to make use of a larger dataset and build a regression model.

---

[12] Pew Research Center, Global Threats Report, July 14, 2015, http://www.pewglobal.org/files/2015/07/Pew-Research-Center-Global-Threats-Report-TOPLINE-FOR-RELEASE-July-14-2015.pdf

The offensive reaction is measured using information on which states are suspected of possessing offensive cyber capabilities. Unfortunately, because governments are highly secretive of their cyber weaponry, this is an area where data is most scarce. Some headway has been made however into documenting the cyber military organizations that governments worldwide are establishing as they prepare for engagement in the cyber warfare domain. We use the findings from one report published by the Wall Street Journal, which identifies 29 such states with "formal military or intelligence units dedicated to offensive cyber efforts."[13] Because the information comes from a media source there may be issues regarding its reliability including a potential omitted data bias if there are excluded states with offensive, albeit unknown, capabilities. This variable consequently represents only a small part of our analysis.

We are also limited to what data we can use for the analysis of levels of cyber defenses but data is available from the World Bank/Netcraft[14] on one particular indicator, that is, the numbers of web servers utilizing encryption methods in each country. The acquisition of secure internet servers is a standard cyber security measure which involves the use of Secure Socket Layer (SSL) technologies to encrypt the data being communicated between a web server and a client, which would otherwise be sent as plain text. Encryption of data adds a layer of security and makes it more difficult for sensitive information to be stolen. SSL's are therefore a service that private firms and banks as well as governments and military organizations have an interest in purchasing to improve their cyber defense against hackers.

If states are concerned about the risk of cyber attacks one way in which they may respond is to encrypt their data, but we are well aware that is only one method of cyber security and our analysis cannot shed light on the many other approaches. Good cyber hygiene practices in one area may or may not spill over to others areas but we are limited by the availability of data indicators in the cyber field and so this question remains unresolved. We are also aware that changes in the secure server variable do not necessarily signify a direct government policy as the private sector plays a major role in securing a country's networks. In this regard we are not solely testing government reaction but also of businesses nationwide. This in fact better reflects the reality of cyber incidents which are often targeted against private firms. The secure server indicator therefore also connects well with the threat perception variable which gauges the fear among the population as a whole, not just from the government.

[13] D. Paletta, et al., *"Cyberwar Ignites a New Arms Race."* Wall Street Journal, October 11, 2015, http://www.wsj.com/articles/cyberwar-ignites-a-new-arms-race-1444611128
[14] World bank/netcraft, Secure Servers per 1 million people, November 1, 2015, http://data.worldbank.org/indicator/IT.NET.SECR.P6

Perceptions versus the Reality of Cyber Threats

Before turning to the key question of the reaction to threat levels, we first examine the extent to which this fear is based in the reality of actual cyber incidents. Figure 1 graphs each country's victim–initiator ratio in their cyber incidents using the incidents dataset for rival states between 2001 and 2011 (Valeriano and Maness 2014) by their perception of cyber threat. This shows whether the frequency of actual cyber actions on the country has a bearing on the levels of concern about the issue.

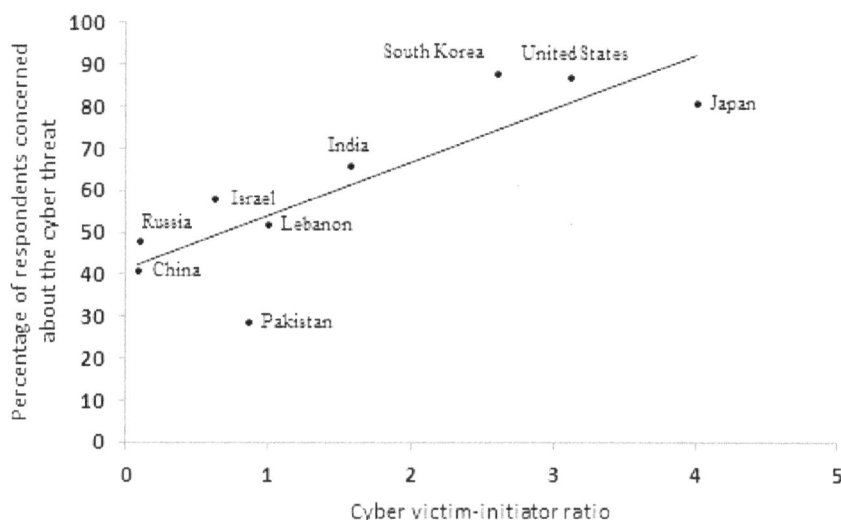

Figure 1: Cyber incidents and threat perception

There is evidently a rough correlation and positive relationship between the two variables. States like China, Russia, and Israel, which tend to be the initiator of cyber actions, have the lowest levels of threat perception, while Japan, South Korea, and the United States have more frequently been victims and consequently have greater concern about cyber actions. This would suggest that fear in the cyber domain is to at least some extent based in the reality of actual cyber incidents.

Of course, the data does not follow a perfectly linear pattern because of the other factors to consider in accounting for heightened fear. The frequent media coverage of cyber incidents for one likely serves to inflate the threat but this is a question that cannot be addressed further here. As we now go forward in investigating the reaction, we know that threat perception likely has some basis in real events with the potential to affect government and/or private sector cyber security policy.

The Perceptions and the Offensive Reaction

A worrying trend observed currently in the international system is that of states developing their offensive cyber capabilities as a means to deter cyber aggression. In its 2011 national cyber strategy, the United States sets out its goal of ensuring "that the risks associated with attacking or exploiting [their] networks vastly outweighs the potential benefits."[15] But as we know from decades of IR research, engaging in power politics as a means of deterrence is only likely to lead to counter reactions, security dilemmas, and the escalation of hostilities (Vasquez 1993). Indeed, Craig and Valeriano (2016) provide evidence that certain states are engaged in competitive cyber relationships based on action–reaction dynamics, these sorts of relationships often escalate in the conventional sphere.

Here we test whether greater cyber fear is more likely among offensively capable states as identified by the Wall Street Journal. If these developments are a reaction to the cyber threat, a correlation would be expected between threat perception and the presence of these offensive capabilities. Table 1 compares the mean level of threat perception between two groups: states that reportedly have offensive cyber capabilities and states where there is no evidence of such developments. The data sample is limited to the 49 countries included in the survey. To determine if the difference is statistically significant, a *t* test is run which tests the null hypothesis that there is no statistically significant difference in means between the two groups.

Table 1: Comparison of mean threat perception between offensive/non-offensive states

	States without offensive capabilities ($N = 22$)	States with offensive capabilities ($N = 17$)
Mean percentage of respondents concerned about cyber threat	55.6	65.7
	$t = 2.16$, degrees of freedom = 37, $p = .037$	

Perceptions of the cyber threat were on average 10.1 percentage points greater in the countries with offensive cyber capabilities, with a mean level of threat perception of 65.7%. The average percentage of people concerned about the cyber threat in countries that did not possess offensive capabilities was 55.6%. The *t* test gives a significant result with a *p*-value of 0.037 meaning the null hypothesis can be rejected and we can confirm that the states with offensive capabilities are statistically more likely to have higher levels of threat perception. This finding is consistent with the proposition that states are

---

[15] The White House, International Strategy for Cyberspace, May 2011, https://www.whitehouse.gov/sites/default/files/rss_viewer/international_strategy_for_cyberspace.pdf

reacting to increased threat through offensive strategies. The correlation also fits within traditional IR theory which sees military build-ups as resulting from external threats, whether perceived or real (Richardson 1960).

Nevertheless, bivariate tests like this cannot establish a causal link between the two variables, and there is always the possibility of intervening factors or a reverse causal mechanism which better explains the correlation. Neither do we know if these findings can be generalized to the entire population of states in the system due to the limited sample. Yet because the evidence fits with theory and expectations it is not unreasonable to suggest that increased levels of threat are motivating the build-up of offensive cyber capabilities. Clearly there is room for further research in this area.

The Perceptions and the Defensive Reaction

The problem comes when offensive solutions are advanced before basic defensive improvements. While the quip that the best defense is a good offense has become conventional wisdom at this point, the veracity of this statement in the world of cyber security is dubious. If states are indeed reacting to the threat by preparing for cyber warfare through offensive capabilities, the next question to ask is if states are also improving their cyber defensive infrastructure in accordance with perceived threats. While it is nearly impossible to fully protect any network, there are steps that can be taken to ensure internal cyber hygiene. One standard method of cyber security is the acquisition of secure web servers. Secure servers are those that encrypt the data being transmitted by using Secure Socket Layer (SSL) technology. The numbers of secure servers is used as our dependent variable as we measure how states have reacted to the cyber threat. The data runs from 2003 to 2014, and in this analysis we often use the standardized measure of the number of secure servers per million of the country's population to make the data more comparable between countries. Figure 2 describes the trends in the secure server data by category of economic development.

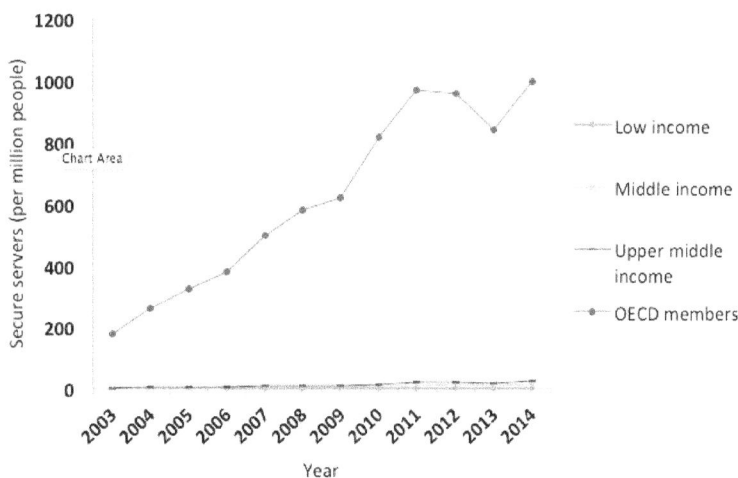

Figure 2: International trends in secure server acquisition

Numbers of secure servers have generally been on an upward trajectory due to increasing internet usage and IT infrastructure over time. What is very noticeable is that the numbers of secure servers seemingly relate to economic development, with OECD countries far exceeding less developed states in numbers of secure servers as well as in their rate of acquisition. Encryption technology is evidently more prevalent in wealthier societies where there are greater numbers of businesses with the capacity to afford such cyber security measures, as well as the more advanced levels of internet infrastructure found in developed economies generally. Poorer countries are evidently failing to catch up with the security practices of wealthier states.

As stated previously, unlike a government's move to establish cyber warfare units, increases to secure servers may not represent a direct government policy but rather a societal reaction. The data measures the number of secure servers across the whole country and so their values depend greatly on the general level of cyber security across society, including the actions of private businesses and organizations. Governments nevertheless can encourage better cyber security measures and enact legislation supporting or demanding such improvements. For example, the 2011 national cyber strategy of South Korea published in the same year as a major cyber incident from North Korea on government websites called on the public and private sectors to encrypt and back up their data.[16] This policy's potential impact is illustrated in Figure 3 which shows that the number of South Korean secure servers in relation to its population has more than doubled within a year, rising from 1128 per million people in 2010 to 2496 per million people in 2011.

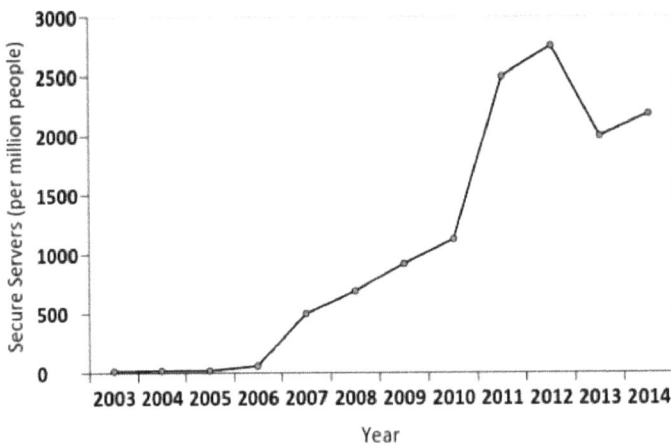

Figure 3: Secure servers in South Korea

---

[16] A. Schweber, *"South Korea Develops Cyber Security Strategy,"* Intelligence, August 28, 2011, http://blogs.absolute.com/blog/south-korea-develops-cyber-security-strategy/

In the following analysis we use threat perception as the independent variable and secure servers as the dependent variable. Figure 4 shows the plot of the relationship between threat perception and secure servers per million people in the year 2014, the closest available year in the dataset to the year the survey was taken.

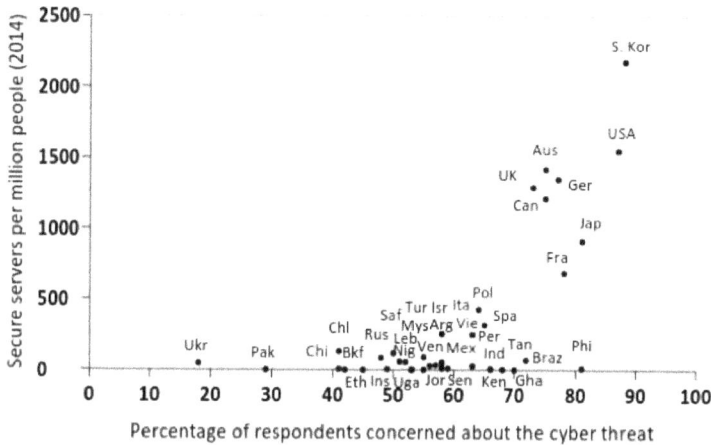

Figure 4: Threat perception and secure servers (2014)

The scatter plot suggests a weak positive relationship between threat and secure servers. States like South Korea and the United States with high levels of threat perception have many more secure servers than states like Ukraine or Pakistan with less fear of cyber attacks. Threat may not necessarily be driving secure server increases however. The relationship may work in reverse in that countries with more secure servers are attacked more frequently and therefore have heightened perceptions of threat. Because greater number of secure servers is symptomatic of a more economically and technologically developed country, such countries may be at greater risk of intrusions from outside hackers. Furthermore, a country with more secure servers is necessarily a more "connected" country with extensive networks and internet usage meaning that cyber methods will be generally more successful than if they were targeted against a less connected country. These factors are likely to result in comparably greater levels of threat perception.

As we are interested in measuring a reaction, instead of using the absolute values the average annual change in secure servers is also calculated for each country. Figure 5 shows the relationship between countries' levels of threat perception and the level at which they tend to increase their secure servers.

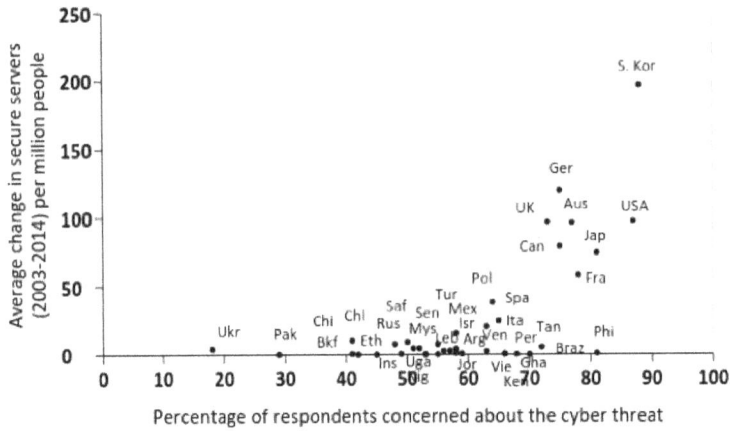

Figure 5: Threat perception and secure server change (2003–2014)

The picture is remarkably similar to Figure 4 demonstrating how closely correlated overall numbers of secure servers are with their rate of acquisition. In other words, states with more secure servers tend to increase them in larger amounts, demonstrating a growing popularity of encryption methods among the developed countries.

Figure 5 shows that larger average increases in secure servers are associated with higher levels of threat perception. At the lower end of the spectrum we see Ukraine, where cyber was a major concern for <20% of respondents and where secure servers have tended to increase very minimally. At the other extreme, South Korea has increased its secure servers by an average of almost 200 per million people in each year and has accordingly experienced the highest levels of threat. But there is evidently a split in the data sample in that for certain states the change in threat perception has no bearing on their secure server acquisition. Many of these countries in which the relationship does not hold appear to be the less developed. They may lack the resources to invest in improving their cyber security and this is a factor that even a high degree of threat perception will be unable to alter. For the more developed countries on the other hand, threat perception and secure servers seem to be more positively correlated.

Despite the relationship we cannot conclude that the threat is *causing* states to increase their secure servers and other factors may better explain the relationship. A possibility is that economic development is an intervening variable explaining both high levels of threat perception, because richer countries are more frequently targeted, as well as explaining levels of secure servers as was previously demonstrated. In other words, the correlation between fear and secure servers may not be a result of states responding to threat, but rather a result of economic development making states ripe targets whilst also being the cause of greater numbers of internet servers.

To investigate further we use an alternative survey data source to determine if the relationship still holds. In Figure 6, we use the 2014 Eurobarometer survey on cyber security[17] as the independent variable which asks respondents from the 28 EU member states their views on the cybercrime threat. We use the data on respondents who "completely agreed" that the threat of cybercrime was increasing. This is a separate question from the last source because it asks about cybercrime as opposed to cyber attacks. Our selection of EU threat data will help control for the influence of economic development as EU states have relatively good levels of development. That potential intervening variable is therefore being kept more constant. One may even expect a stronger relationship when using this cybercrime survey data because the encryption of data via secure servers is particularly applicable to issues of online theft.

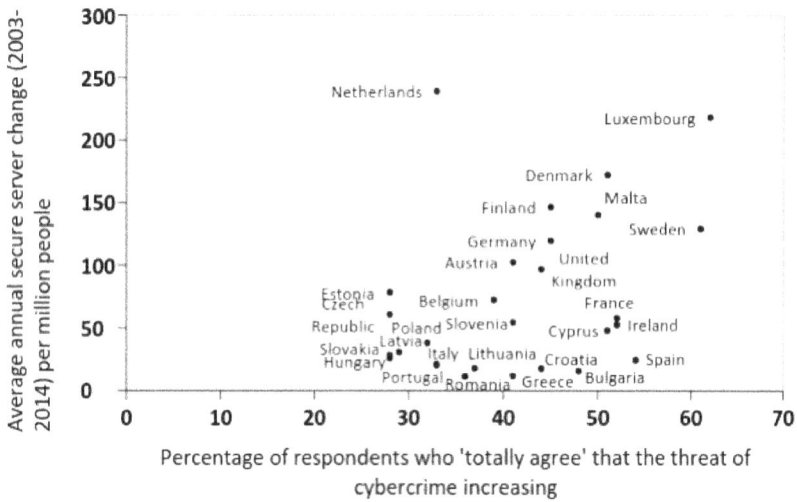

Figure 6: Cybercrime threat perception and secure server change (2003–2014)

Figure 6 highlights the weakness of the relationship between threat and defensive infrastructure developments. The data points do not follow a consistent pattern to enable us to identify a correlation. Although some states may be responding to levels of threat, many other states in the sample are evidently not doing so. Maybe this is evidence that many states and private organizations are failing to take the cyber security issue seriously. Moreover, we see states like the Netherlands, an outlier, having the highest changes in secure servers but relatively low levels of threat perception within the population, suggesting that the reasons for increasing cyber security measures are broader than simply levels of threat.

---

[17] European Commission, Special Eurobarometer 423: Cyber Security, February 2015, http://ec.europa. eu/public_opinion/archives/ebs/ebs_423_en.pdf

We can approach our research question from another angle by operationalizing the dependent variable in terms of percentage change as opposed to absolute increases. Using percentage change will measure the increase in secure servers relative to the state's pre-existing secure servers and thus is more useful for modeling the increased effort invested into improving cyber security. It will also control for our previous finding that economically developed states tend to have larger absolute increases. Accordingly, Figure 7 plots the relationship between threat, using the original PEW data, and the average annual percentage change in secure servers from 2003 to 2014.

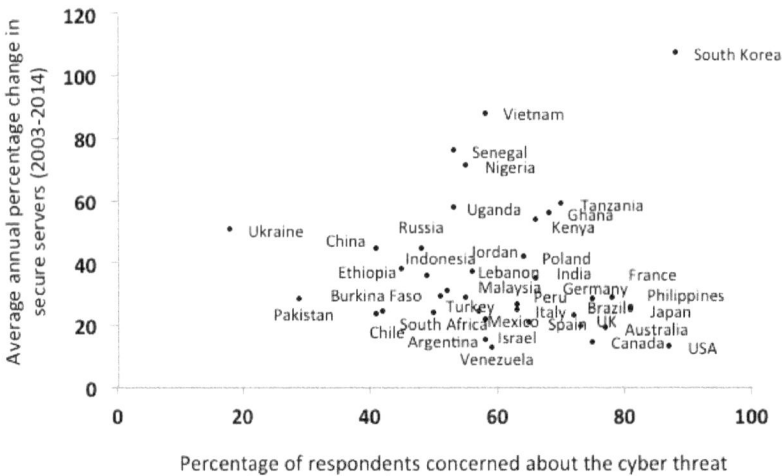

Figure 7: Threat perception and secure server percentage change

When using percentage change the results become very different. Where there was a correlation before, now there is no such identifiable trend in the data with dots widely spread. Heightened fears about cyber attacks are not associated with greater secure server growth rates. Perhaps only a few states are responding to the threat in this way such as South Korea, which in accordance to its very high perception of threat as a result of continual cyber incidents from the North has the greatest secure server growth in the sample. With 88% of respondents concerned about the threat, South Korea has on average more than doubled its numbers of secure servers each year. Yet the data shows that this certainly does not apply to the sample generally.

To analyze this further, a *t* test is conducted to ask if there is a statistically significant difference in means between two groups: states with below average secure server percentage growth and states with above average secure server percentage growth over the whole period. The results are shown in Table 2.

Table 2: Threat perception and secure server growth (2003–2014)

	Below-average secure server growth ($N = 30$)	States with offensive capabilities ($N = 17$)
Mean percentage of respondents concerned about the cyber threat	61.1%	56.4%
	$t = 0.80$, degrees of freedom = 37, $p = 0.43$	

Going against some of the previous findings, states with above average percentage growths in secure servers from 2003 to 2014 had in fact lower average levels of threat perception than states with smaller growth rates, although the result is not statistically significant with a p-value of 0.43. This analysis has shown that, when measuring secure servers by percentage change rather than absolute increases, there is no suggestion that threat is driving states to put increased efforts into improving their cyber security infrastructure.

Nevertheless, this does not settle the issue regarding the previously observed finding that there was a correlation between threat perceptions and secure servers. The possibility that this was explained by intervening variables was raised but this cannot be confirmed with the limited survey data we have. To gain a larger sample size with more explanatory power, we instead use data on cyber incidents (Valeriano and Maness 2014) and build a statistical model to account for numbers of secure servers. This method allows us to control for other variables in order to help isolate the independent effect that being the victim of a cyber incident has on cyber security infrastructure.

We use a panel dataset of 64 countries observed from the years 2003 to 2012 and run a fixed-effects regression model. This technique controls for country specific effects which may correlate with the independent variables. The country sample is determined by two factors. Firstly, only countries involved in ongoing interstate rivalries are included due to the nature of the incidents dataset. The second condition is that these countries must also have cyber security programs as these are the countries with the capacity to coordinate a response and are therefore of most interest when investigating the dynamics within the cyber domain. These countries are determined by the UNIDIR cyber index[18] which identifies countries with notable cyber security policy developments within their military or civilian sectors.

Our dependent variable is the number of secure servers a country possesses per one million of its population, and the three control variables included are: GDP per capita[19] in thousands of US dollars, to account for the economic development that has been previously shown to explain levels of cyber security; military spending measured

---

[18] UNIDIR, *"The Cyber Index: International Security Trends and Realities,"* March 2013, http://www.unidir.org/files/publications/pdfs/cyber-index-2013-en-463.pdf
[19] World Bank, GDP per capita, November 1, 2015, http://data.worldbank.org/indicator/NY.GDP.PCAP.CD

in billions of US (constant 2011) dollars[20]; and the levels of internet penetration in society, indicated by the numbers of internet users per 100 people.[21] Stronger military powers may be expected to invest more into cyber security to protect their critical infrastructure and military networks, and clearly more internet users in a country necessarily entails more servers, so these are factors that should also be controlled for.

The key independent variable is whether or not the state was victim to a cyber incident within the past 2 years of the year under observation, thereby giving sufficient time to observe a reaction. Cyber incidents data is used instead of the survey data because it provides us with not only cross sectional but time series data, thereby increasing the sample size for use in a more sophisticated statistical model. The regression will predict the effects of each independent variable on a state's numbers of secure servers while holding constant the impact of the other variables. This therefore allows us to get a better idea of whether cyber threats on their own motivate the acquisition of secure servers.

Table 3: Fixed effects regression on secure servers (2014) per million people

Variable	Coefficient (std. error)	*p*-value	95% Confidence interval	
Internet users	6.75 (.95)	0.000	4.88	8.62
GDP per capita	22.69 (6.64)	0.001	9.64	35.74
Military expenditure	2.91 (1.05)	0006	0.85	4.97
Cyber victim	−16.36 (52.40)	0.755	−119.29	86.56
(Constant)	−455.35 (104.48)	0.000	−660.59	−250.11

[20] Stockholm International Peace Research Institute, Military Expenditure Data, October 27, 2015, http://www.sipri.org/research/armaments/milex

[21] World Bank, Internet Users per 100 people, November 1, 2015, http://data.worldbank.org/indicator/IT.NET.USER.P2

Table 3 shows the results of the fixed effects regression model on the number of secure servers (per million people), using a sample size of 604. The number of internet users in a country was a significant predictor of the number of secure servers. An increase of 1 internet user per 100 people is associated with 6.75 more secure servers per million people. GDP per capita is also significant, and an increase of 1000 dollars per person is associated with 22.7 more secure servers per million people. Military spending is also positively and significantly correlated with more secure servers. A 1 billion increase in military expenditure is associated with having 2.9 more secure servers per million people. Although statistically significant, these are not very large effects in real terms. The R^2 value of 0.43 indicates that 43% of the variance in the data is being accounted for by the model, and there are clearly more variables to consider when trying to explain levels of encryption technology in a state.

Our key variable of interest is whether a country was a victim of a cyber incident in any of the two previous years as this might be a critical indicator of heightened awareness of the cyber threat to a state's national security. Our analysis is sufficient to show that this indicator is not a significant predictor of the number of secure servers. The relationship is negative but not statistically significant, suggesting that the previously observed correlation between cyber threat and secure servers was spurious, and better explained by other factors such as economic development.

Summary

We first provided evidence supporting the claim that states are reacting to their cyber threat concerns by developing offensive cyber capabilities. This is consistent with the cyber arms race proposition. States in which the public had greater fear of cyber attacks were more likely to be making offensive preparations. This is worrying because it suggests that the security dilemma in cyberspace is driving states toward more confrontational policies as a means to achieve security.

What would be even more concerning is if this was occurring at the expense of basic cyber hygiene domestically. We investigated this question by looking into the specific practice of securing web communications via encrypted servers. Because much of the cyber threat relates to the unauthorized access into private networks and theft of sensitive data, secure servers are an important as well as relatively basic cyber security measure. Acquisition of such technology would appear to represent the initial step that can be taken toward establishing basic levels of protection and hygiene that are needed in an internet connected society. Despite this, our statistical investigation suggests that the cyber threat whether real or perceived does not in and of itself motivate states to increase their nationwide cyber security infrastructure in this way.

Although we initially uncovered a correlation between heightened threat among a population and increased secure servers the use of alternative measurement techniques gave different results, and when controlling for other variables there was no statistically significant relationship. Overall, it appears that the acquisition of secure servers is not driven by how threatened the country feels in the cyber realm.

Despite positive albeit weak correlations between secure server increases and threat perception, it seems there may be intervening variables like economic development at play. Indeed, the regression results indicate that GDP per capita as well as military spending, and internet penetration, are more significant predictors of secure servers than past experience of cyber incidents.

Conclusion

This research has helped to provide a macro picture of cyber security practices in the global system, and how they may relate to perceptions of the cyber threat to national security. If states are indeed reacting to their security concerns through mainly offensive cyber warfare preparations, it raises worrying prospects for international relations. The escalatory potential of the global cyber arms build-up should be of great concern to scholars working on these issues. More work is needed on how the security dilemma and action reaction processes operate in this domain, as well as its implications for interstate cyber conflict.

On the other hand, we have not seen much evidence that states are taking the necessary steps to ensure their own internal protection against growing threats. Data encryption is of course only one method of protection, but we are unfortunately constrained as to what data is available. It is very possible that states are reacting defensively to the threat by other means. Future research will examine this possibly with both data sources and qualitative methods.

Attempts to boost cyber security throughout wider societal projects are difficult for governments who lack control over the private sector. Regardless of levels of threat, a lack of cooperation between governments and private business will likely hinder any substantial improvements to a country's cyber defenses. In fact, private sector-led improvements in cyber security might be more effective than government-directed efforts. Unfortunately, such questions are beyond the scope of the data analyzed here but our study nonetheless points to the idea that states, in the face of increased threats, are not doing all they can to build networks that can withstand attack in the first place.

Acquiring layers of defense is moreover only one model for a cyber security strategy, and the debate may be moving toward the concept of resilience rather than defense. Determined hackers will likely always find a way in and adopting a strategy of resilience would instead involve the ability to anticipate attacks and recover systems quickly in order to minimize damage and disruption.

Empirical research in cyber security is only in its nascent era. Our modest effort is an attempt at what we hope others in the field will seek to accomplish, which is to uncover the dynamics of cyber security processes by analyzing evidence rather than focus on the pronouncements and bluster that so often pervade the cyber domain. More considered and careful data work must be undertaken because this domain is critical. Beyond its potential military uses, the opportunity for cyber connectivity to embolden education, research, business, and commination is clear.

References

Clarke, Richard A., and Robert Knake. 2010. *Cyber War: The Next Threat to National Security and What to Do About It*. NY: Harper Collins.

Craig, Anthony J. S., and Brandon Valeriano. 2016. "Conceptualizing Cyber Arms Races." *Submitted to the 8th International Conference on Cyber Conflict*. Tallin, Estonia: NATO Cooperative Cyber Defence Centre of Excellence, June 1–3, 2016.

Diebert, Ronald. 2011. "Tracking the Emerging Arms Race in Cyberspace." *Bulletin of the Atomic Scientists* 67 (1): 1–8.

Dunn Cavelty, Myriam. 2012. "The Militarisation of Cyberspace: Why Less May Be Better." *Presented at the 4th International Conference on Cyber Conflict*, eds C. Czosseck, R. Ottis, and K. Ziolkowski. Tallinn, Estonia: NATO Cooperative Cyber Defence Centre of Excellence, June 5–8, 2012.

Fahrenkrug, David T. 2012. "Countering the Offensive Advantage in Cyberspace: An Integrated Defensive Strategy." *Presented at the 4th International Conference on Cyber Conflict*, eds C. Czosseck, R. Ottis, and K. Ziolkowski. Tallinn, Estonia: NATO Cooperative Cyber Defence Centre of Excellence, June 5–8, 2012.

Gibler, Doug, Toby J. Rider, and Michael Hutchison. 2005. "Taking Arms Against a Sea of Troubles: Conventional Arms Races During Periods of Rivalry." *Journal of Peace Research* 24 (2): 251–276.

Gortzak, Yoav, Yoram Z. Haftel, and Kevin Sweeney. 2005. "Offense-Defense Theory: An Empirical Assessment." *Journal of Conflict Resolution* 49 (1): 67–89.

Glaser, Charles L., and Chaim Kaufmann. 1998. "What is the Offense-Defense Balance and Can we Measure it?" *International Security* 22 (4): 44–82.

Hammond, Grant T. 1993. *Plowshares into Swords: Arms Races in International Politics, 1840–1991* (Columbia: South Carolina Press).

Huth, Paul, and Bruce Russett. 1990. "Testing Deterrence Theory: Rigor Makes a Difference." *World Politics* 42 (4): 466–501.

Jensen, Benjamin, Ryan C. Maness, and Brandon Valeriano. 2016. "Cyber Victory: The Efficacy of Cyber Coercion." *Presented at the Annual Meeting of the International Studies Association*.

Jervis, Robert. 1978. *Perception and Misperception in International Politics* (Princeton, NJ: Princeton University Press).

Kello, Lucas. 2013. "The Meaning of the Cyber Revolution: Perils to Theory and Statecraft." *International Security* 38 (2): 7–40.

Liff, Adam P. 2012. "Cyberwar: A New 'Absolute Weapon'? The Proliferation of Cyber Warfare Capabilities and Interstate War." *Journal of Strategic Studies* 35 (3): 401–428.

Lindsay, Jon R. 2013. "Stuxnet and the Limits of Cyber Warfare." *Security Studies* 22 (3): 365–404.

Richardson, Lewis F. 1960. Arms and Insecurity: A Mathematical Study of the Causes and Origins of War, ed. Nicolas Rashevsky and Ernesto Trucco, (Pittsburgh: The Boxwood Press)Rid, Thomas. 2013. *Cyber War Will Not Take Place* [Kindle], London: C Hurst & Co Publishers Ltd.

Sample, Susan. 1997. "Arms Races and Dispute Escalation: Resolving the Debate." *Journal of Peace Research* 34 (1): 7–22.

Valeriano, Brandon, and Ryan Maness. 2014. "The Dynamics of Cyber Conflict between Rival Antagonists, 2001–2011." *Journal of Peace Research* 51 (3): 347–360.

Valeriano, Brandon, and Ryan C. Maness. 2015. *Cyber War versus Cyber Realities* (New York: Oxford University Press).

Valeriano, Brandon, and Ryan C. Maness. 2016. "Caution in the Cyber Realm: The Inadequacy of Deterrence Frameworks." Presented at the Annual Meeting of the Midwest Political Science Association, Chicago, IL.

Vasquez, John A. 1993. *The War Puzzle* (Cambridge: Cambridge University Press).

Wallace, Michael D. 1979. "Arms Races and Escalation: Some New Evidence." *Journal of Conflict Resolution* 24 (2): 289–292.

Arming Cyberspace: The Militarization of a Virtual Domain

Miguel Alberto N. Gomez[A]

The increasing frequency of offensive cyberspace operations (OCOs) directed toward states, particularly the disclosure of Stuxnet in 2010 that appears to have been aimed at disrupting Iran's nuclear development program, has prompted a reassessment of state behavior in cyberspace. In the years since, states have gradually militarized cyberspace through the establishments of various programs that have framed this as a new domain of warfare. Yet despite the pace of these transformations, a unified theoretical understanding of this phenomenon continues to remain conspicuously absent. To date, scholars have attempted to explain such by highlighting the advantages offered by cyberspace while others have cited the growing fear-based rhetoric grounded by the increasing societal dependence on technology. Neither of these, however, can adequately explain why certain states have militarized while others have not despite predictions of such taking place. Consequently, this study, encompassing the period from 2011 to 2014, proposes that depolarizing these respective arguments may close the existing theoretical gap. In doing so, the study employs a quantitative analytical approach that examines how cyberspace had been militarized across states as a function of both strategic considerations and resource requirements which are both driven by rational choice and societal perceptions regarding this domain.

Keywords*: analysis, counterinsurgency, critical thinking, and operational environment*

Introduction

In the first decade of the twenty-first century, the discourse concerning cyber security in the global security landscape has shifted from criminal acts toward specific political and/or military events. Most notably, the discovery of the Stuxnet worm in June 2010 overturned previously held beliefs regarding offensive cyberspace operations (OCOs) (Farwell and Rohozinski 2011; Liff 2012a; Sanger 2012).

Stuxnet, believed to have been the first instance of a weaponized malware, was found to have caused disruptions in Iran's nuclear centrifuges at the *Natanz* facility (Farwell and Rohozinski 2011). Although the use of cyberspace in conjunction with on-going conflicts between states had not been novel at this point, this was the first instance wherein physical damage was deemed possible through actions in the virtual world. This signaled a reevaluation of the nature of events in cyberspace in terms of

[A] Assistant Professorial Lecturer, De La Salle University

doi: 10.18278/gsis.1.2.4

their professionalism, intent, and increasing complexity (Cavelty 2012; Valeriano and Maness 2013). In so doing, these changes support the *cui bono* logic of attributing these activities to states or state-sponsored organizations.

Consequently, the nature of these events assigns responsibility for responding to a state's civil defense and military apparatus (Cavelty 2012). Furthermore, the increasing number of suspected state or state-sponsored OCOs are believed to have accelerated the militarization of cyberspace with the adoption of military doctrines specific to this domain, the emergence of national cyber strategies, and the establishment of military units responsible for conducting warfare in cyberspace (Cavelty 2013; Luiijf and Besseling 2013; Ottis 2009; Nye 2014; Young 2009).Consequently, this study defines militarization as the adoption of cyberspace by the military in either an offensive or defensive manner (or both). As of 2013, however, of the 114 states with existing cyber programs, less than half (47) have involved their military—the remaining 67 have developed exclusively civilian programs (UNIDIR 2013).

If the threat of state or state-sponsored OCOs targeting critical infrastructure is indeed on the rise and if the actor task with responding to such is the military (Cavelty 2012), then what accounts for the varying levels of militarization across states? Simply stated, why do some states choose to militarize cyberspace to meet this perceived existential threat while others do not?

The existing literature provides two arguments that serve to explain this phenomenon. The first recognizes that the rising societal dependence on technology introduces an existential threat that may be exploited by states and thus requires cyberspace to be secured (Barnard-Wills and Ashenden 2012; Bendrath 2001; Hansen and Nissenbaum 2009; Starr 2009).[1] The second acknowledges the advantages that the cyber domain offers relative to land, air, and sea. Most notably, its asymmetric nature, plausible deniability, and its offensive advantage are factors for militarization (Libicki 2009; Liff 2012a; Saltzman 2013; Sharma 2010). While both offer probable reasons why states would choose to militarize cyberspace, certain realities remain unaccounted for.

Although technology has indeed become commonplace in the political, economic, and military spheres, we have yet to find a case wherein OCOs have been used in a catastrophic attack against critical infrastructure. At most, only partial and temporary disruptions were achieved (Lawson 2013; Rid 2012). For example, the case of Estonia in 2007 that resulted in the disruption of the financial and government services, while vast in scale was eventually contained without any long-term economic or financial damage.

With regards to the latter, although there are indeed advantages offered by this domain, both Iasiello and Valeriano point out that most instances of such have been viewed by their targets as mere nuisance and thus far have failed to coerce their targets as intended (Iasiello 2013; Maness and Valeriano 2015). Although Stuxnet in 2010 was claimed to have damage some of Iran's nuclear centrifuges, this had not hindered their

---

[1] The current cyber strategy released by the U.S. Department of Defense has dropped such alarmist language though (Farrell 2015).

enrichment program in the long run (Iasiello 2013). Furthermore, Chinese activities in cyberspace—although mostly in the form of cyber espionage—do not give credence to the argument that the attribution problem associated with cyberspace encourages its use (Passeri 2015). As argued by Valeriano and Maness, activities in cyberspace can be attributed to specific actors with a certain degree of confidence based on pre-existing rivalries and national interests (Valeriano and Maness 2015).

In light of the absence of a suitable explanation for state behavior in cyberspace, this study attempts to bridge the existing theoretical gap that does not account for the continued militarization of this domain despite the lack of success in using OCOs to shape state policies as a function of either technological capabilities or societal dependence. Specifically, the study posits that an understanding of the phenomenon depends not on a strict adherence to one of the aforementioned explanations. Rather, the study shows that the choice to militarize this domain is a function of both its technological advantages relative to other domains (e.g., land, sea, and air) and by the capabilities developed in response to perceived risk.

Consequently, the study is organized as follows. The succeeding section presents the reader with the theoretical framework adopted by this study. From this point, the study moves forward to discuss the specific methodology in use. This section also includes a brief discussion regarding the analytical approach applied to the study. The succeeding sections then present an analysis of the data collected as well as the result of the applied quantitative methods. The final section summarizes the results of the study and provides future direction for scholars wishing to expand on the results presented here within.

Theoretical Framework

To account for the variation of militarization across states requires a reassessment of the explanations offered by existing theories rather than seeing these as either invalid or mutually exclusive. In doing so, it must be acknowledged that the degree to which cyberspace is militarized is dependent on both strategic goals and the availability of resources rather than simply the ability or the need to use such resources for the sake of doing so (Gartzke 2013; Liff 2012a). This argument finds support in a number of studies. For instance, Valeriano and Maness have shown its frequent use among states that have pre-existing rivalries (Valeriano and Maness 2013). Their analysis suggests that states with existing regional rivalries use cyberspace as a means of signaling during periods of increased tension (Maness and Valeriano 2015).

In addition, both Andres and Axelrod further investigated the influence of rivalries vis-à-vis strategic objectives. Andres coins the term *inverted-militarized-diplomacy* in which policy makers utilize militarized assets (i.e., cyber weapons) to seize desired resources (e.g., proprietary information) while relying on diplomats to limit escalation (Andres 2014). Parallels can be drawn with the English use of privateers to challenge the position of Spain during the Elizabethan period. Since these individuals were not visibly agents of the English crown, the uncertainty resulting from this limited the possibility of escalation. Similarly, Axelrod and Iliev have developed a mathematical model predicting when states would engage in the use of cyber weapons. A crucial factor in such a decision is the expected gains relative to the resources invested in the development and use of such. Simply put, actors will only chose to utilize these assets if the expected gains is substantial enough to justify (1) the loss of the ability to re-use them (i.e., zero-day exploits) and/or (2) the possibility of escalation (Axelrod and Iliev 2014). This builds on the points raised by the previous authors arguing that strategic considerations provide the initial rationale for the militarization of this domain. As such, the following hypothesis is proposed:

H1: *States that experience a greater number of offensive cyberspace operations from rival states attain a higher level of militarization.*

While the literature supports the idea that strategic interests are crucial in militarizing cyberspace, one must also take into account the consequences of militarization. Liff argues that while states may have the technical capabilities and strategic interests to militarize cyberspace, the decision to do so is constrained by their conventional capabilities (Liff 2012a). This argument rests on two important points. First, cyberspace is a resilient domain. While states may engage in OCOs to weaken their rivals, whatever damage incurred is temporary—the nature of cyberspace limits, if not denies, the possibility of permanent damage to a target (Maness and Valeriano 2015). This perspective is grounded in the resilient nature of this domain coupled with declining costs associated with technologies that allows for the development of systems that, while still vulnerable, can be restored within a defined amount of time. Sharma points to this argument to account for the limited use of cyberspace as an instrument of warfare (Sharma 2010).

Second, the availability of a conventional option (e.g., an air strike) allows an aggressor to better signal his intent given the resilient nature of cyberspace (Lawson 2013; Liff 2012b; Stone 2013). This extends the previous point by arguing that gains achieved through actions in cyberspace are temporary and any further consolidation would require intimidation or coercion through other means. Stone argues that parallels may be drawn between the use of cyberspace and airpower during the Second World War wherein these act as complementary tools to other instruments of warfare (i.e., ground forces) (Stone 2013). Furthermore, Liff supports this argument by suggesting that conventional capabilities are needed to secure gains made in the cyber domain (Liff 2012a). As such, the following hypothesis is proposed:

H2: *States that attain greater hard power reach a higher level of militarization.*

While strategic considerations may contribute to the militarization of cyberspace, states intending to do so would require resources to support this undertaking. Furthermore, the mobilization of these resources has been achieved through fear-based rhetoric on the part of elites. Lawson posits that perceptions regarding societal dependence on technology contribute to the perceived existential threat originating from cyberspace (Lawson 2013). These threats are rooted at both the societal and technological levels given how this domain is viewed as both technological and societal constructs. As proposed by Barnard-Wills and Ashenden, cyberspace is built on networking information technologies that form the foundations of a domain that is shaped by the manner that *people and institutions, think, understand, and talk about this space* (Barnard-Wills and Ashenden 2012). Both the technological and social components are understood to have their own vulnerabilities that, in turn, introduce risk that need to be mitigated (Giles and Hagestad 2013; Hansen and Nissenbaum 2009). In her study, Cavelty identifies the use of the military and other civil defense organizations in responding to catastrophic attacks against critical infrastructure—the targets most often cited as those facing the greatest risk (Cavelty 2012). As such, the following hypotheses are proposed:

H3: *Increasing societal use of cyberspace increases militarization.*

H4: *Increasing technological risk associated with cyberspace increases militarization.*

Even if this two-tiered perception of cyberspace is accepted, the impact of the risk associated with cyberspace rests on its resonance across a wider audience. In her study, Cavelty identifies one of its referent objects as critical infrastructure (Cavelty 2012). Catastrophic attacks aimed at these would prompt their securitization. Furthermore, Hansen and Nissenbaum have identified three specific modalities under which such a securitization takes place: *hypersecuritization, everyday security practices, and technifications.* The first refers to large-scale disaster scenarios as a result of societal dependence on information and communication technology (ICT). While the second relates to how threats originating from cyberspace would impact an individual's day-to-day life (Hansen and Nissenbaum 2009). To be viewed as an existential threat, Sharma argues that the impact of activities in cyberspace must span these two modalities (Sharma 2010). While no single case has proven these scenarios as of yet, elites have employed these scenarios to call for the further militarization of cyberspace (Lawson 2011). As such, the following hypothesis is proposed:

H5: *Elite influence through speech acts increases militarization.*

It should be noted that this framework does not discount current explanations that are grounded on the advantages offered by this domain and by the existential fear surrounding it, but instead synthesizes these by insisting that the act of militarization does not occur independent of other factors. The militarization of this domain is mandated by a strategic need to do so and is enabled by the availability of resources as determined by the elite's ability to instrumentalize risk associated with the use of this domain.

Methodology

Case Selection

Given that no suitable dataset currently exists to capture the variation of cyberspace militarization across states, this study has constructed its own by utilizing a variety of open-source resources and is comprised of 88 unique observations. Given that militarization is viewed at the level of the state, the universe in question involves states with existing cyber programs. As of 2013, the United Nations Institute for Disarmament Research (UNIDIR) has identified a total of 114 states with existing cyber programs involving both the private and public sectors (UNIDIR 2013). In addition, the time period considered is from 2011 to 2014. The lower bound is set to 2011 as a result of changes in perception in response to the discovery of the Stuxnet worm in 2010. The data is lagged by 1 year to allow this to take effect. Furthermore, authors such as Cavelty observe that events such as Stuxnet have altered the perception of cyberspace from being a civilian domain to that of a military one (Cavelty 2013). Consequently, extending the study earlier than 2011 is not insightful given this change.

The cases sampled from this universe are instances of states that have an existing cyber program and have experienced OCOs attributed to either state or state-sponsored actors. The sampling strategy adopted is crucial for two reasons. First, by omitting cases attributed to cybercrime, the amount of noise from unrelated events is reduced. Second, threats originating from these state or state-sponsored actors result in the state being the referent object as oppose to cybercrime that affects individuals or private organizations, respectively (Cavelty 2013). Information regarding specific instances of OCOs are obtained from the *Hackmageddon* project—an open-source initiative that tracks cases of cybercrime and cyber warfare through multiple sources (e.g., news articles and industry reports) on a monthly basis (Passeri 2015). To identify valid instances of state or state-sponsored OCOs from this repository, the methodology proposed by Ottis is applied (Ottis 2009). All the identified cases that match the above-mentioned criteria are then aggregated to the level of the state.

It should be pointed out that two important (and inherent) limitations exist. First is reporting bias. The nature of these events limits the possibility of such reaching the public. Consequently, there is the possibility of underreporting the actual number of incidents that take place at the state level. The choice to rely on open sources allows for the broadest and most reasonable coverage. Second, the challenge of attributing the source and target of OCOs limits the accuracy of the data. Although Valeriano and Maness suggest that the existing interstate relationships could limit this problem, there continues to be no method to definitively identify actors short of aggressors and targets willingly disclosing information (Valeriano and Maness 2015).

Operationalization

In order to account for variations in cyberspace militarization, the dependent and independent variables represented in the previously defined hypotheses must be operationalized. Although the study employs pre-existing metrics to represent these variables, a number of these have been developed solely for this study due to the lack of existing metrics.

Cyberspace Militarization (Dependent Variable)

To date there are no existing studies that suggest a quantitative measure for the militarization of cyberspace. Consequently, this study employs artifacts that have been identified to be crucial for the military's involvement in cyberspace (Luiijf and Besseling 2013; Ottis 2009; Young 2009). These are as follows:

- A military doctrine or policy regarding cyberspace (d).
- A national cyber security strategy that recognizes state or state-sponsored cyber threats (s) and.
- A military and/or civilian unit(s) involved in to cyber defense and/or offense (u).

Each component is assigned a specific value and a weighted score is computed based on Equation 1. As the literature does not provide insight as to the precise weight to be given for each component, the study employs a near equal weighting scheme with an exception toward military doctrine or policy that is identified as playing a significant role (Young 2009). To this end, the components of this variable are scored based on the scheme indicated in Table 1.

It should be noted that the study is constrained by the availability of information in the public domain. Sources include the ETH Defense White Papers and National Security Strategies Series (ETH 2015), the NATO Cooperative Cyber Defense Center of Excellence (NATO CCDCOE 2015), the European Union Agency for Network and Information Security (ENISA 2015), the UNIDIR's Cyber Index report (UNIDIR 2013), and Luiijf and Besseling's study on national cyber security strategy (Luiijf and Besseling 2013).

Table 1. Militarization Scoring

Component	Score	Description
Military doctrine/policy	(1)	Has a dedicated doctrine/policy that recognize cyberspace as a unique domain of warfare or as a source of existential threats
	(0.5)	Has a separate doctrine/policy where cyberspace is recognized as a domain of warfare or as a source of existential threats
	(0)	Has no doctrine/policy that recognizes cyberspace as a domain of warfare or as a source of existential threats
National cyber security strategy	(1)	Has an existing national strategy recognizing state or state-sponsored OCOs as a threat
	(0.5)	Has an existing national strategy but does not recognize state or state-sponsored OCOs as a threat
	(0)	Has no existing national strategy
Cyber units	(1)	Has an existing military organization responsible for cyberspace
	(0.5)	Has an existing civilian organization responsible for cyberspace
	(0)	No existing organization responsible for cyberspace

$$\text{militarization} = d(0.4) + s(0.3) + u(0.3)$$

Equation 1. Cyberspace Militarization

Rivalry

To operationalize *H1*, the study employs dyadic rivalries between states that have experienced OCOs are identified using Klein's rivalry dataset (Klein 2006). While the dataset only covers periods up to 2001 (possibly limiting its reliability), the results from Valeriano and Maness' study that employed this dataset as well (encompassing periods from 2001 to 2011) appear to demonstrate its validity and reliability with respect to conflicts in cyberspace (Valeriano and Maness 2013). In measuring the significance of rivalry, the percentage of OCOs experienced from rivals relative to the total number of OCOs observed is used (see Equation 2). In cases where the sources of attacks could not be attributed, the study records this as having originated from a nonrival.

$$\text{rivalry} = \text{CNOs from Rivals} \div \text{Total CNOs}$$

Equation 2. Rivalry

Hard Power

To operationalize *H2*, the study employs national power as measured using the Composite Index of National Capability (CINC) present in the *Correlates of War version 4* dataset (Sarkees and Wayman 2010). While CINC is primarily a measure of hard power, it should not limit its validity since the existing literature refers specifically to conventional military capabilities when referring to state power vis-à-vis cyberspace (Liff 2012b). It should be noted, however, that the most recent CINC values are only until 2007.

ICT Use

To operationalize *H3*, societal dependence on ICT is captured through the *use sub-index* of the International Telecommunications Union's (ITU) *ICT development index*. The *use sub-index* measures the current usage of ICT within a given society and is a compounded score that integrates other measures such as *fixed broadband subscription, Internet access*, etc. (ITU 2013; 2014). The study employs the mean of this measure from 2011 to 2014.

Risk

As with militarization, there is currently no quantitative state-level measure for risk in cyberspace. To operationalize H4, the study applies the risk measurement formula (see Equation 3) usually employed by private organizations (SANS Cyber Defense 2012). For this study, the mean of malware infection rates from 2011 to 2014 per state is used as a proxy measure for threat, vulnerability, and impact. The presence of an infection is a manifestation of these three concepts (Microsoft Corporation 2015). These rates are based on infections identified in devices running Microsoft's operating system (Myslewski 2014). Given that the organization has >80% of the market share globally, this is an acceptable measure. The mean of Internet usage from 2011 to 2013 as measured by the ITU serves as the proxy for impact, the assumption being that the presence on the Internet increases the number of possible victims of infection (World Bank 2014). At the state level, the ITU's 2014 Global Cyber Security Index best represents countermeasures for these threats (ITU & ABI Research 2014). The result is then scaled from 0 to 1.

$$risk = (threat \times vulnerbaility \times probability \times impact) \div countermeasures$$

Equation 3. Risk

The result of the above-mentioned formula represents what is referred to as residual risk or the amount of risk faced once the necessary steps to mitigate threats have been applied.

Elite Influence

Of the variables involved in this study, measuring the influence of elite speech acts is challenging to quantify. Moreover, there are no consolidated records concerning elite references to cyberspace. To operationalize *H5*, the ratio between references of elite and nonelite statements concerning policy change is used as a proxy. This measures the importance of the topic vis-à-vis the specific actor (GDELT Project 2013). These values are obtained through the *GDELT Project* that monitors broadcast, print, and web-based news sources and to date has over a quarter of a billion entries (Leetaru 2015). The primary limitations faced are the scope of information available to the *GDELT Project* as well as the accuracy of its automated systems that are used to classify the relevant actors in these documents.

Polity

The additional variable of polity from the *Polity IV* dataset that measures the level of democracy in a given state is applied as a control variable (Marshall, Gurr, and Jaggers 2010). Hare points out that regime type may impact how a state perceives threats from cyberspace (Hare 2010). Consequently, this may shift the referent object away from the state as noted by Cavelty (Cavelty 2013). The study employs the mean of the *polity 2* indicator from 2011to 2014.

Analytic Approach

To confirm the possible causal relationship between the dependent (*Militarization*) and independent (*hard power, risk, ICT use,* etc.) variables that account for the variation of cyberspace militarization, the study adopts a two-step quantitative approach.

To trace causal paths between the variables, the study implements a Bayesian Causal Network (BCN) to provide a graphical representation of the causal links between variables. The use of BCNs allow for (1) a graphical output that is easy to interpret, (2) a measure that shows a positive, negative, or absent causal relationship, and (3) mitigates the impact of small sample bias (Kalisch and Mächler 2011). BCNs, however, do not offer a measure of the statistical significance. Furthermore, certain BCN techniques require that there be no hidden variables and that all variables involved in the causal relationship have been accounted for. Although this may appear to be constrictive, this prerequisite demands that the theoretical framework be as rigorous as possible and serves to ensure robust results.

Once the causal structure has been established through the previous method, the study then applies cluster analysis. The reason for this is twofold. First, if the previously established causal links are valid, then what should result are unique clusters in which the respective values of both dependent and independent variables are unique for each cluster—thus confirming the previous findings. For the purpose of this study, the expectation maximization (EM) clustering algorithm is employed as it accounts for the possibility unobserved variables (Bilmes 1998). This is meant to address the constraints imposed by the first stage in the analysis. Second, aggregating individual states into unique clusters allows for the analysis of how dependent variables vary across these groups. Since clustering maximizes the difference between clusters while minimizing differences among its members, this results in each cluster representing a unique case with each cluster member (i.e., state) serving as individual observations. This allows for the possibility of applying qualitative techniques such as the method of similarity/difference to confirm the causal relationships. The difference between variables across clusters is measured through a simple two-group t test on their respective means.

Once the validity of these clusters is established, it confirms the causal relationship derived by the first step. The result would then either support or refute the proposed hypotheses that explain the process of the militarization of cyberspace.

Results and Analysis

Summary Statistics

The resulting dataset produced for this study identifies 88 unique states with existing cyber programs that had also experienced OCOs within the defined period. Table 2 presents the summary statistics of the dataset and from this, several key observations are made. Beginning with the level of militarization across states it can be stated that while most states have engaged in one form of this or another, there is as of yet no global trend toward the militarization of cyberspace. With a mean of 0.447 and by analyzing the specific components of the scores relevant to this variable, it can be said that most states have focused on establishing military and/or civilian units that are responsible for cyberspace in response to their respective cyber security strategies.

Table 2. Cyberspace Militarization Summary Statistics

	Mean	Median	Maximum	Minimum
Risk	0.119	0.073	1.000	0.000
ICT use	3.757	3.632	8.233	0.217
Hard power	0.011	0.003	0.200	0.000
Elite influence	0.609	0.624	1.000	0.078
Rivalry	0.148	0.000	1.000	0.000
Polity	4.966	8.000	10.00	-10.00
Militarization	0.447	0.450	1.000	0.000

There are, however, fewer states (41%) whose existing military doctrine recognize cyberspace as a unique domain of war. This suggests that despite the growing number of OCOs attributed to state or state-sponsored actors, less than half believe this to be a new domain of warfare. A similar pattern is seen with regards to their respective national cyber strategies wherein only 31% acknowledge state and state-sponsored OCOs.

Moving the discussion forward, several key observations can also be established regarding the independent variables. Concerning the risk faced by states, the sample shows this to be skewed to the right. Its distribution, along with a mean value of 0.12 and a median on 0.07 suggests that, despite the perception of increasing risk, most states have been able to mitigate threats from cyberspace. Moreover, the fact that *ICT use* and *elite influence* appears to be normally distributed (see Figure 1) in the sample suggests the absence of bias in favor of states that are better able to address threats from cyberspace as an explanation for how *risk* has been represented or elites that have ardently vocalized the need to secure this domain. In addition, the mean value of 3.76 and maximum value of 8.23 for *ICT use* also suggests that despite the increasing societal dependence on these technologies it cannot, as of yet, be said to be pervasive at a global level. Consequently, it may be argued that the perceived threat originating from the technological component of cyberspace has yet to reach a critical point, thus accounting for the level of militarization captured by this dataset.

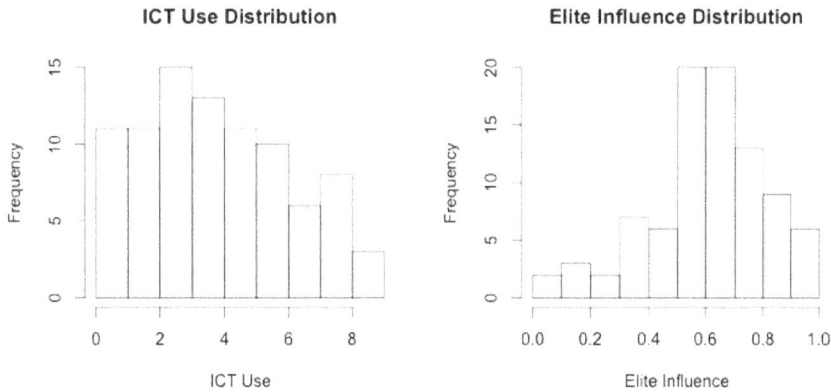

Figure 1. ICT Use and Elite Influence Distribution

Interestingly, the variable *Polity* appears to be skewed to the left while that of *Hard Power* is skewed to the right (see Figure 2). Although authoritarian regimes are represented in the data, the majority of the observations are of democratic regimes. In addition, most of the observations suggest middling to weak military capabilities (i.e., Hard Power). These two points are crucial, particularly in the context of Hare's study wherein such states are vulnerable to highly disruptive OCOs that target their critical infrastructure (Hare 2010). If this is the case, Cavelty's model predicts further militarization of cyberspace (Cavelty 2013). Following this line of reasoning, if militarization is a function of both *Polity* and *Hard Power* alone, then one should expect a higher mean value for this variable.

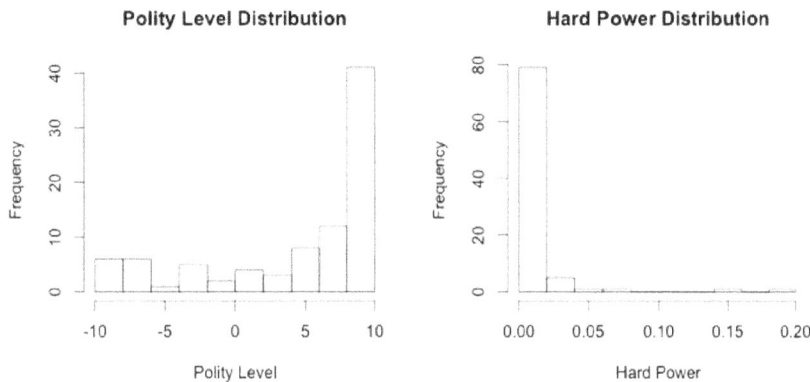

Figure 2. Polity and Hard Power Distribution

Finally, it should be noted that fewer instances of OCOs originating from rivals have been observed in contrast with Valeriano and Maness' study. This deviation could be explained by the manner in which the population was sampled compared to the previous study. For Valeriano and Maness' dataset, only cases of state initiated actions were included in the dataset. Instances of state-sponsored activities were kept at a minimum (Maness and Valeriano 2015). In doing so, the sampling may have been indirectly limited to states with prominent rivalries, thus accounting for the characteristic of this variable in their study.

Causal Relationship

Before proceeding with reviewing the causal relationship between the dependent and independent variables, additional information may be gleaned by inspecting how these are associated with one another. Table 3 shows the respective correlation coefficients (Pearson's Correlation) along with their *p* values.

Table 3. Correlation Table

Independent Variables	Dependent Variable	Correlation Coefficient	p Value
Risk	Militarization	−0.433	2.575e−5
Rivalry	Militarization	0.070	5.183e−1
Hard Power	Militarization	0.435	2.280e−5
Elite Influence	Militarization	−0.026	8.113e−1
ICT Use	Militarization	0.472	3.356e−6
Polity	Militarization	0.285	7.128e−3

With the confidence interval set to 0.95, it can be seen that only *risk, hard power, ICT* use and *polity* are statistically significant in terms of their relationship with *militarization*. The latter three can be said to be positively associated with *militarization* while the former (*risk*) is negatively associated. If applied to the current hypotheses, the association displayed by *hard power* and *ICT use* appears to conform to the expectations of *H2* and *H3* that suggest the expected behavior of these two variables. On the other hand, *risk* appears to contradict H4 that expects a positive association between *militarization* and *risk*. This, however, could be explained by the manner in which this variable was operationalized. Since the metric is obtained by using existing countermeasures as the divisor, lower risk suggests greater capabilities in cyberspace. These capabilities may be re-tasked or re-developed to support the militarization of this domain, thus explaining the negative relationship. Finally, the coefficients and *p* values of the remaining variables suggest a lack of association between these and the dependent variable, possibly discrediting hypotheses *H1* and *H5*. However, since correlation does not imply causation, further tests are required to evaluate the hypotheses.

Table 4. Causal Relationship vis-à-vis *Militarization*

Variables	Linked to *Militarization*	Causal Strength
Risk	Yes	−0.765
ICT use	Yes	0.053
Hard power	Yes	4.080
Elite influence	No	−0.032
Rivalry	No	0.058
Polity	No	0.011

The outcome of generating a BCN is seen in Table 4. The first column on the left-hand side identifies the independent variables. The second indicates whether or not there is a direct causal link between the independent variables and the dependent variable (*militarization*). The right-most column lists the respective strength of the causal link between the dependent and independent variables. In this case a value of zero (or near zero) would indicate an absence of a causal relationship. A positive or negative value for this column indicates the direction of the causal relationship. From Table 4, several relevant observations can be established. First, the absence of a link between the variables measuring *rivalry, elite influence*, and *polity* and that of *militarization* suggest that these variables do not contribute to the emergence of this phenomenon. Referencing the association of *rivalry* and *elite influence* to that of *militarization* in Table 3, the previous step (correlation) had already shown an absence of a relationship. Furthermore, the causal strength between these two variables to that of the dependent variable (see Table 3) are near zero, thus indicating an absence of such a relationship and any immediate causal influence. This, however, does not indicate that these variables do not play an indirect role in the militarization of this domain. Expanding the dataset by including more observations may change the result given the probabilistic nature of BCNs.

Second, both variables measuring *risk* and *hard power* appear to have a direct causal relationship with that of *militarization*. The previous analysis of the association between these two variables to that of the dependent variable coincide with the direction and causal strength indicated in Table 4. It illustrates the negative relationship between *risk* and *militarization* and the positive relationship with that of *hard power*. Curiously, *ICT use* that had a significant association with *militarization* has a near zero value in Table 4. This suggests that while there appears to be a causal link between *ICT use* and *militarization*, it is not as significant as the other two variables. Simply stated, *ICT use* is not prominent enough to significantly influence the militarization of cyberspace but still contributes to the militarization of cyberspace in some way. But as with the previous point, the influence that *ICT use* may play may change assuming that these tests are redone with a greater number of observations.

Result Verification

At this point, the inferred causal relationship appears to confirm *H2, H3*, and *H4* (represented by *hard power, risk*, and *ICT use*, respectively) while rejecting the remaining hypotheses. In effect, the initial results support the proposition that both strategic considerations and risk perception directly influence the variation of cyberspace militarization. However, confirming the causal links can only be achieved if the relevant variables on a state level are clustered such that unique values of *militarization* would emerge in the resulting groups. The result of which can be seen in Table 5.

Table 5. Cluster Summary

Group Number	Group Size	Risk	ICT Use	Hard Power	Militarization
1	7	0.023	5.047	0.077	0.864
2	67	0.091	3.499	0.005	0.429
3	14	0.299	4.345	0.001	0.325

In keeping with the inferred causal chain, three groups with unique levels of *militarization* are present.[2] These three groups may be classified as having high (0.67–1), medium (0.34–0.66), and low (0–0.33) militarization of cyberspace. It should be pointed out that in the process of evaluating the uniqueness of each group with one another, *ICT use* had been shown to not be statistically unique across the groups. This finding reinforces the weak causal strength that was previously established for this variable and allows for the rejection of *H3*.

In contrast, the measures for *risk* and *hard power* vary across these three groups and serves to explain the respective levels of *militarization*. Beginning with Group 1 that is represented by the United States, this has the highest level of *militarization* among the three groups. Most notably, this group's variables measuring *risk* and *hard power* are the lowest and highest among the three, respectively. The level of risk associated with members of this group suggests significant capabilities in mitigating cyber-borne threats. If compared to that of the other groups, the militarization of cyberspace decreases as risk increases—confirming earlier findings. While this does not immediately prove *H4*, as this hypothesis requires risk to be high for militarization to follow in the same direction, it may be argued that as risk increases, the steps taken to reduce such would require an investment in technologies and processes that could, in turn, be used to increase the militarization of cyberspace. As such, *H4* cannot be rejected.

In addition, it is also observed that as the value of *hard power* is reduced so does that of *militarization*. Again, this confirms the previous findings and is aligned with hypothesis *H2*, thus this hypothesis is retained.

---

[2] The variables for each group have been subjected to *t* tests to evaluate whether they are statistically different from one another.

The interaction between *risk* and *hard power* is made more apparent if compared across the three groups. Starting with the case of Group 1 and Group 2, there is a stark difference between *risk* (by a factor of 4) and *hard power* (by a factor of 15). While it could be said they are experiencing comparable levels of risk, the conventional military capabilities of Group 1 is significantly higher than that of Group 2 and could account for the higher value for *militarization*. In contrast, Group 2 and Group 3 have nearly identical levels of *hard power* but the risk faced by Group 2 is less than the latter by a factor of 3 and could account for the latter's lower levels of *militarization*.

Table 6. Inter-Group Similarities

Group Number	Risk	ICT	Power	Militarization
1		X		
2		X		X
3		X		X

Apart from the rationale derived from the causal chain that had been previously established. The resulting values for the level of cyberspace militarization could also be accounted for by Liff's model seen in Table 7. It should be pointed out that this model only takes into account the conventional military capabilities of the said actors and does not explicitly account for the risk faced in cyberspace. To integrate risk in the process of militarization, the model developed by Hare is relevant but requires one to reconsider the possible influence of polity—acknowledging the correlation identified earlier in this section. This model is illustrated in Table 8.

Table 7. State Interactions (Liff 2012a)

State Interaction	Characteristics
Strong state versus superpower	• OCOs provide only marginal advantages and useful only for difficult to attribute attacks against civilian or military infrastructure • A superpower may perceive vulnerability in cyberspace and may not initiate aggression • OCOs act as a counter-force or counter-value weapon against conventional capabilities
Weak state versus strong state/ superpower	• Weak state lacks the ability to follow through from the OCO with conventional attacks • Weaker state could launch OCOs against stronger adversary but is limited due to fear of possible escalation through conventional means • OCOs from strong state/superpower may not occur due to lack of targets in cyberspace
Weak state versus weak state	• Lack of conventional capabilities would shift conflict over to cyberspace • Limited conventional capabilities would limit escalation

Table 8. Cyber Vulnerabilities and Types of States (Hare 2010)

		Socio-Political Cohesion (C)	
		Weak (W)	**Strong (S)**
Power (P)	**Weak (W)**	De-stabilizing political actions in cyberspace, attacks on Internet Infrastructure, criminal activities	DDoS and other major attacks on critical-infrastructure
	Strong (S)	De-stabilizing political actions in cyberspace	Criminal activities in cyberspace

With these models on hand, the proposed relationship between risk and hard power are further strengthened. Starting with Group 1 and Group 2, the first mode of interaction could be use to explain the current level of militarization (see Table 7). As both groups face relatively comparable levels of risks (see Table 6), the greater conventional capabilities of Group 1 states would prompt these to view cyberspace as an alternative platform from which to initiate aggression and would thus invest in this domain. In contrast, Group 2 with lower conventional capabilities would militarize cyberspace as a means to counter possible aggression from Group 1 states. In terms of the risk these two groups face, Group 1 is classified under the P-S/C-S quadrant while Group 2 would be considered in the P-W/C-S quadrant based on Table 8. In both these cases, the solutions required to mitigate these are similar to one another and could thusly explain the similar values for risk between these two groups.

In contrast, the relationship between Group 2 and Group 3 follows the second interaction more closely. The greater conventional capabilities of Group 2 could influence it to develop additional capabilities in cyberspace. Group 3, on the other hand, would invest limited capabilities in cyberspace due to either (1) technological limitations or (2) fears of possible retaliation from stronger states. Lower levels of *militarization* for Group 3 could also be attributed to the risk it faces. Using Hare's model in Table 8, Group 3 states would be found in the P-W/C-W quadrant wherein similar threats from the other quadrants are present, but with the addition of de-stabilizing political actions. What this suggests is that rather than investing in external capabilities aimed toward other states, Group 3 states could focus instead on internal security and censorship (Giles and Hagestad 2013; Hare 2010).

Collectively, the quantitative analysis provided in conjunction with Hare and Liff's models explain how both *risk* and *hard power* could influence the level of *militarization*. But where then does this leave the growing use of ICT? Although it cannot be denied that there continues to be a gap between the prevalence of ICT between certain states (ITU 2014), this disparity does not appear to account for the choice to militarize cyberspace. This is to say, greater societal dependence on such technologies does not result in the militarization of this domain. The fact that relatively few states have included cyberspace in their respective military doctrines supports this claim. A better explanation as to why *ICT use* does not appear to significantly influence *militarization* is the uniform nature of the underlying technologies.

While the degree of use may differ from one society to another or between states, the manner in which such technologies function remain to be the same. A computer in the United States does not operate differently from one in Russia. The difference lies in the ability of certain actors to better understand how these technologies function in order to maximize their use. Phrased differently, the intellectual capability of a society may matter more than the prevalence of ICT. This argument finds support in the fact that, as the data shows, states that face lower risk (through better countermeasures) have a higher level of *militarization*. Furthermore, one has also to take into account the degree with which ICT has been integrated into society. As shown in Table 2, most states have adopted a moderate level of *ICT use*. This suggests that the level of dependence on these technologies have yet to reach a point wherein cyberspace may be used as a means to inflict wide-ranging damage as perceived by Sharma (2010). Consequently, these two reasons could account for the level of similarity and the low degree of influence this variable has on the process of militarization.

Conclusions and Future Direction

The growing number of OCOs being attributed to state or state-sponsored actors demands a better understanding of the underlying factors that result in the militarization of cyberspace. While the existing literature posits two seemingly incompatible arguments centered on either fear-based rhetoric or rational choice, the study has demonstrated that both these factors account for the varying levels to which cyberspace has been militarized across states.

On the one hand, while increasing societal use of information communication technologies have led to greater risks associated with these technologies, the capabilities developed that are necessary to mitigate such could similarly lead to the transform the domain of cyberspace for use in warfare. Aside from the re-tasking of defense technologies, there is now the appearance of technologies once associated with the criminal elements of cyberspace in OCOs attributed to state or state-sponsored actors. The malleability of this technology supports the argument that increasing use alone does not account for the militarization of this domain, but rather the ability to maximize the functionality provides those with this skillset to expand beyond the traditional domains of air, land, and sea.

Equally important—and thus linking the two existent theories—is the continued relevance of conventional military capabilities vis-à-vis the use of cyberspace. While there is no doubt as to the advantages offered by this virtual domain, namely its asymmetric characteristics, low cost of entry, and challenges of attribution; these exist in conjunction with the stated policy goals of a state. The ability to employ this domain is dependent on conventional military capabilities to consolidate whatever gains were obtained in the process. Although it would be theoretically possible to utilize OCOs to disrupt a state's critical infrastructure in times of war, the impermanence of the damage caused requires additional resources to be brought to bear in order to force a change in policy or behavior of a given adversary.

Viewed as the causal explanations for the militarization of cyberspace, the risk faced by a state may be understood as the catalyst that encourages the militarization of this domain. However, without conventional military capabilities that could be used to apply constant pressure on one's adversaries, viewing OCOs as a *revolution in military affairs* is of limited value.

With this in mind, what role do the other aspects (e.g., regime type, rivalry, and elite influence) identified by the literature have on militarization? Although the study has not demonstrated that these to have a direct causal influence on militarization, this does not suggest that no relationship exists. As previously mentioned, the nature of the quantitative techniques applied could lead to differing results if the number of observations is increased. Regime type, for instance, could influence the type of risk faced by states and, in turn, influence the technologies developed to meet these risk. Hare's model captures this and is seen clearly in cases of states such as that of the United States and the People's Republic of China (PRC). The former perceives threats to its critical infrastructure and other services in cyberspace. Consequently, this prompts the development of technologies to ensure resilience and pro-active prevention of disruptive events. The latter, in contrast, is concerned with dissent and political activism in cyberspace. Consequently, this results in the emergence of censorship technologies that do not translate directly to offensive capabilities in cyberspace—though espionage-related capabilities would benefit from these (Giles and Hagestad 2013; Hare 2010).

Similarly, perceived risk originating from internal threats could account for the decision to engage (or not) in OCOs against other rival states. However, cases such as that of the PRC do not follow this line of reasoning as the most prominent of their activities in this domain have been directed against their military, political, and economic rivals.

Lastly, the influence of elites in the militarization of this domain could, in the view of authors such as Nissenbaum, be constrained by a lack of understanding of its nature and the continued lack of synergy between experts in technology and national policy (Hansen and Nissenbaum 2009). This would lead to a situation wherein political elites could, and do, vocalize the dangers posed by cyberspace but lack the proper understanding of how to apply these technologies as a tool to support national policies and goals.

The manner in which states conceptualize cyberspace at this point in time finds parallels with that of the mid-twentieth century and the advent of nuclear war. While the technology of the time offered to revolutionize warfare, few understood the implications of such and the extent with which these would alter the relationship between states and their respective military strategies.

References

Andres, Richard B. 2014. "Inverted-Militarized-Diplomacy: How States Bargain with Cyber Weapons." *Georgetown Journal of International Affairs* 4: 119–129.

Axelrod, Robert, and Rumen Iliev. 2014. "Timing of Cyber Conflict." *Proceedings of the National Academy of Sciences* 111 (4): 1298–1303. doi:10.1073/pnas.1322638111.

Barnard-Wills, D., and D. Ashenden. 2012. "Securing Virtual Space: Cyber War, Cyber Terror, and Risk." *Space and Culture* 15 (2): 110–123. doi:10.1177/1206331211430016.

Bendrath, Ralf. 2001. "The Cyberwar Debate Perception and Politics in U.S. Critical Infrastructure Protection The Information Society as Risk Society." *Information & Security* 7: 80–103.

Bilmes, Jeff a. 1998. "A Gentle Tutorial of the EM Algorithm and Its Application to Parameter Estimation for Gaussian Mixture and Hidden Markov Models." *International Computer Science Institute* 4 (510): 126. doi:10.1.1.119.4856.

Cavelty, Myriam D. 2012. "The Militarisation of Cyberspace?: Why Less May Be Better." In 4th International Conference on Cyber Conflict, eds C. Czosseck, R. Ottis, and K. Ziolkoswki. Tallinn, Estonia: NATO CCD COE, 141–153.

Cavelty, Myriam D.. 2013. "From Cyber-Bombs to Political Fallout: Threat Representations with an Impact in the Cyber-Security Discourse." *International Studies Review* 15 (1): 105–122. doi:10.1111/misr.12023.

ENISA. 2015. "National Cyber Security Strategies in the World." https://www.enisa.europa.eu/activities/Resilience-and-CIIP/national-cyber-security-strategies-ncsss/national-cyber-security-strategies-in-the-world.

ETH. 2015. "Defense White Papers and National Security Strategies." http://www.isn.ethz.ch/Digital-Library/Publications/Series/Detail/?id=154839.

Farrell, Henry. 2015. "What's New in the U.S. Cyber Strategy?" *The Washington Post.* http://www.washingtonpost.com/blogs/monkey-cage/wp/2015/04/24/whats-new-in-the-u-s-cyber-strategy/.

Farwell, James P., and Rafal Rohozinski. 2011. "Stuxnet and the Future of Cyber War." *Survival* 53 (October): 23–40. doi:10.1080/00396338.2011.555586.

Gartzke, Erik. 2013. "The Myth of Cyberwar: Bringing War in Cyberspace Back Down to Earth." *International Security* 38 (2): 41–73. doi:10.1162/ISEC_a_00136.

GDELT Project. 2013. "GDELT—Data Format Codebook v1.03." GDELT Project.

Giles, Keir, and William Hagestad. 2013. "Divided by a Common Language?: Cyber Definitions in Chinese, Russian and English." In *5th International Conference on Cyber Conflict*. Tallinn, Estonia: NATO CCD COE, 413–429.

Hansen, Lene, and Helen Nissenbaum. 2009. "Digital Disaster, Cyber Security, and the Copenhagen School." *International Studies Quarterly* 53 (4): 1155–1175.

Hare, Forrest. 2010. "The Cyber Threat to National Security Why Cant We Agree." In *Conference on Cyber Conflict* ed C. Czosseck and K. Podins. Tallinn, Estonia: CCS COE Publications, 211–225.

Iasiello, Emilio. 2013. "Cyber Attack: A Dull Tool to Shape Foreign Policy." In *5th International Conference on Cyber Conflict*. Tallinn, Estonia: NATO CCD COE, 451–468.

ITU. 2013. "Measuring the Information Society Report." Geneva, Switzerland: ITU.

ITU. 2014. "Measuring the Information Society Report." Geneva, Switzerland: ITU.

Kalisch, Markus, and M. Mächler. 2011. "Causal Inference Using Graphical Models with the R Package Pcalg." *Journal of Statistical Software* 47 (11): 1–26.

Klein, J.P. 2006. "The New Rivalry Dataset: Procedures and Patterns." *Journal of Peace Research* 43 (3): 331–348. doi:10.1177/0022343306063935.

Lawson, Sean. 2011. "Beyond Cyber-Doom: Cyberattack Scenarios and the Evidence of History." *Mercatus Center George Mason University Working Paper* 11-01 (2011).

Lawson, Sean. 2013. "Beyond Cyber-Doom: Assessing the Limits of Hypothetical Scenarios in the Framing of Cyber-Threats." *Journal of Information Technology & Politics* 10 (1): 86–103. doi:10.1080/19331681.2012.759059.

Leetaru, Kalev H. 2015. "GDELT Project."

Libicki, Martin C. 2009. "Sub Rosa Cyber War." *In The Virtual Battlefield: Warfare*, eds Christian Czosseck, and Kenneth Geers. Amsterdam: IOS Press, 55–65.

Liff, Adam P. 2012a. "Cyberwar: A New 'Absolute Weapon'? The Proliferation of Cyberwarfare Capabilities and Interstate War." *Journal of Strategic Studies* 35 (March 2015): 401–428. doi:10.1080/01402390.2012.663252.

Liff, Adam P. 2012b. "Cyberwar: A New 'Absolute Weapon'? The Proliferation of Cyberwarfare Capabilities and Interstate War." *Journal of Strategic Studies* 35 (3): 401–428. doi:10.1080/01402390.2012.663252.

Luiijf, Eric, and Kim Besseling. 2013. "Nineteen National Cyber Security Strategies." *International Journal of Critical Infrastructures* 9 (1): 3–31.

Maness, R.C., and B. Valeriano. 2016. "The Impact of Cyber Conflict on International Interactions." *Armed Forces & Society* 42 (2): 301-323. doi:10.1177/0095327X15572997.

Marshall, Monty G., Ted Robert Gurr, and Keith Jaggers. 2010. "Polity IV Project: Political Regimes and Transitions, 1800–2009." *Polity*.

Microsoft Corporation. 2015. "Microsoft Inteligence Report." http://www.microsoft.com/security/sir/default.aspx.

Myslweski. R, 2014. "Windows Hits The skids, Mac OS X On The Rise." *The Register*. http://www.theregister.co.uk/2014/03/15/windows_desktop_and_laptop_market_share_dips_below_90_per_cent/.

NATO CCDCOE. 2015. "Cyber Security Strategy Documents." https://ccdcoe.org/strategies-policies.html.

Nye, Joseph S. 2014. "The Regime Complex for Managing Global Cyber Activities."

Ottis, Rain. 2009. "Theoretical Model for Creating a Nation-State Level Offensive Cyber Capability." In *8th European Conference on Information Warfare and Security*, ed H. Santos. Lisbon, Portugal: ACI, 177–182.

Passeri, Paolo. 2015. "Hackmageddon." http://www.hackmageddon.com/.

Rid, Thomas. 2012. "Cyber War Will Not Take Place." *Journal of Strategic Studies* 35 (3): 5–32.

Saltzman, Ilai. 2013. "Cyber Posturing and the Offense-Defense Balance." *Contemporary Security Policy* 34 (1): 40–63. doi:10.1080/13523260.2013.771031.

Sanger, David E. 2012. "Obama Order Sped Up Wave of Cyberattacks Against Iran." The New York Times.

SANS Cyber Defense. 2012. "Insider Threat Risk Formula: Survivability, Risk, and Threat." Boston, MA: SANS Institute.

Sarkees, Meredith Reid, and Frank Wayman. 2010. *Resort to War: 1816–2007.* Washington, DC: CQ Press.

Sharma, Amit. 2010. "Cyber Wars: A Paradigm Shift from Means to Ends." *Strategic Analysis* 34 (1): 62–73. doi:10.1080/09700160903354450.

Starr, Stuart. 2009. "Toward a Preliminary Theory of Cyberpower." In *Cyberpower and National Security,* eds Franklin Kramer, Stuart Starr, and Larry Wentz. Washington, DC: Potomac Books, 43–88.

Stone, John. 2013. "Cyber War Will Take Place!" *Journal of Strategic Studies* 36 (1): 101–108. doi:10.1080/01402390.2012.730485.

UNIDIR. 2013. *The Cyber Index—International Security Trends and Realities.* New York: UNIDIR.

Valeriano, Brandon, and Ryan Maness. 2014. "The Dynamics of Cyber Conflict Between Antagonists, 2001–2011." *Journal of Peace Research* 51 (3): 347-360.

Valeriano, Brandon, and Ryan C. Maness. 2015. *Cyber War Versus Cyber Realities. Cyber War Versus Cyber Realities.*

Young, Mark D. 2009. "National Cyber Doctrine?: The Missing Link in the Application of American Cyber Power." *Journal of National Security Law & Policy* 7: 173–196.

Applying Robert A. Pape's Denial Strategy to Computer Warfare

Trevor Sutherland

The aim of this study is to use Robert Pape's Bombing to Win as a stepping off point. This article analyzes the utility of computer warfare as a method to coerce states. It then continues on to consider other views on cyber coercion and how actors and targets can be classified. Actors are mapped to one of four quadrants while six separate types of targets are created.

Keywords: *Cyber war, computer network attack, strategic bombing, malware, computers*

In the aftermath of World War I, there was much debate over the future role of the airplane in the military conflict. During the war, it had shown itself to be a platform with much potential, filling a number of roles and assisting the traditional land and sea forces with their missions. At the same time, strategists realized that its incorporation into warfare also enabled forces to undertake missions unlike those that were previously imagined. Rather than simply reconnoitering and spotting for artillery, theorists saw that the airplane could be turned into a flying piece of artillery, enabling the birth of what we now think of as strategic bombing.

After World War I, several thinkers became active in the debate over the use of Airpower. Of the major thinkers in the early interwar period, Giulio Douhet remained today the most widely referenced. Douhet focused mainly on strategies that involved attacking non-military targets such as industry, transportation, and government centers (Ferrari 1942, 179). By attacking targets that would conceivably disadvantage the civilian populations of home countries, Douhet felt that the civilian populations would pressure their governments into submitting to the will of those doing the bombing (Pape 1996, 60). This view was further popularized by the first commander of the British Royal Air Force (RAF), Hugh Trenchard, who began a policy of directly bombing civilian populations based on his experiences policing the British colonies. Both Douhet and Trenchard exemplify the feeling of many early airpower theorists that the airplane is an inherently offensive weapon. They felt that an effective defense would at best be attritional to the attackers and that some forces would inevitably survive to attack their target (Bradbeer 2004, 125).

A similar line of thought dominates the discussions of cyber war that are occurring today. As our daily lives become more interconnected and networked there are simply too many potential vectors for attack. Moreover, as this interconnectedness fosters increased efficiency it stands to reason that interdependency will only increase over time, ultimately putting more systems at greater risk. Most books devoted to cyber security focus on this problem in the civilian sense, either speculating on the

doi: 10.18278/gsis.1.2.5

effects of an attack made against element of infrastructure, like electricity distribution or economic institutions. While there is some evidence that such tactics might have been used to coerce individuals for monetary reasons (Brenner 2011, 557), there is no basis for judging the costs and effects of an attack made on a population as a whole. The general assumption put forward in most books is that the victimized population will cease to be able to effectively function and pressure their government to capitulate to the attacking force. This is very similar to the Douhet model of strategic bombing, in which a civilian population's morale is broken and rendered incapable of effective resistance.

If populations exposed to direct bombing in the past are used as an example, it stands to reason that the expected outcome of civilian capitulation would likely not occur. This strategy, employed extensively during World War II against population in Britain, Germany, and Japan, has since been found to be only moderately useful. While population-targeted coercion can be effective in situations when nuclear weapons are expected to be used, attacking civilian populations more often has an opposite effect. By bringing civilians into the war fighting process, a rally-around-the-flag effect is usually seen increasing resistance rather than undermining it, as was seen in both England during World War II and North Vietnam during the Vietnam War.

Instead, most effective strategies for coercive bombing focus on limiting the military effectiveness of an opponent. This is accomplished through the use of airpower to complicate the manufacture of arms, interdict their transportation to the battlefield, and disrupt communications on the battlefield and within the theater (Pape 1996, 69). To better understand what a coercive action involving the cyber sphere would look like, cyber capabilities should be analyzed in terms of how they can fulfill these goals without effecting the population as a whole.

Is Cyber Coercion Viable?

In *Bombing to Win*, Robert A. Pape examines the use of strategic bombing for coercion. He compares its usefulness for this task against land and sea-based measures and finds that airpower is ideal for coercion for a number of reasons. First, it is flexible and precise, allowing those that use it to better separate actions taken against the military from those taken against the population. Second, it allows greater amounts of ordnance to be put on target with more precision and over a greater area than either land- or sea-based measures. Lastly, unlike land-based coercion, strategic bombing does not require a decisive ground victory to be successful.

The advantages of cyber coercion are similar to those of airpower. Flexibility and precision can be achieved through defining the attributes that are present in a given environment before an attack can begin, as was evidenced in the outbreaks of both the Conficker and Stuxnet worms (Bowden 2011, 56; Falliere, Murchu, and Chien 2011, 7). This would further reduce the risk of collateral damage through misidentification of buildings or the location of any non-military buildings nearby. Payload delivery would also be more efficient in a cyber-coercive campaign, as physical distance and munitions weight are not factors. Lastly, just as aerial coercion does not require ground superiority but only a measure of air superiority, cyber coercion needs neither. What is needed in some situations is "network superiority," the ability to function in an opponent's networks with complete freedom.

The Limitations of Denial

Pape also outlines the limitations of denial, his term for coercion carried out against military targets, in *Bombing to Win*. These are (a) effective denial within the area over which control is sought, (b) constant maintenance of pressure until concession is given, and (c) the ability to control the territory by force (Pape 1996, 32). These limitations present five major problems for cyber operations as they are typically understood today.

First, they require significant tangible effects. While there is proof that the manipulation of industrial control systems and Supervisory Control and Data Acquisition (SCADA) systems can yield spectacular results (Brenner 2011, 1497), these effects are often achieved through negligence on the part of the system operator and can be classified as targets of opportunity. This lack of diligence is seen in the utility of websites such as Shodan.com that act as a "google for SCADA." It is reasonable to assume that a government, especially one that is in a state of heightened conflict, would secure phone, power, and other essential systems quickly. Also, most SCADA systems that are accessible through the Internet are set up for the convenience of those maintaining the system (Bentek Systems 2012). If the networked controllers ever became a large-scale problem, most industrial and manufacturing systems could simply be "unplugged," from the Internet with few consequences.

Other systems are networked through their very nature and these will likely be the most vulnerable over the course of a potential coercion campaign. Such systems include the Internet, air traffic control systems, and the systems that control road and rail travel. For most of these systems there are non-networked alternatives, though these alternatives are less efficient, even after implementation. This loss of efficiency can be seen as a limited form of interdiction, though one not likely to be successful without other factors utilized as well.

The second problem presented by Pape's limitations is the need for persistent pressure. While assets and systems can be rendered inoperable through a cyber attack, once an alternative method of providing the same service has been established the coercive attempt has effectively failed. For a successful outcome, pressure must be maintained over a potentially long period of time. This can be achieved by consolidating control over the target computer networks, allowing for the pacing of operations to slowly degrade systems, which is similar to the actions Stuxnet took against Iranian nuclear processing centrifuges.

Once network superiority is achieved, another option for persistent capability is falsifying and modifying data rather than destroying it. By not deleting the data, the hope is that the target will not notice the extent of the infection, thus enabling the coercer to influence the target over a longer period of time. Of course, it should be noticed that this strategy can cause significant attribution problems if not enacted properly. If actions are unattributable to the coercer through overuse of this subterfuge, then they constitute only wasted effort on the part of the coercer.

Third, the attempt at cyber coercion must be able to resist the target's attempts to undo the long term efforts of the coercer. The basis of cyber security is the realization that every program potential for a critical flaw that can be exploited for disastrous results. This theory applies equally in this case to the coercer and the target. By consolidating control over the target networks, the coercer is opening himself to the potential that his efforts will be flawed in a way that enables the target to take control of his network. While there are ways to minimize this risk, the potential consequences of such an action are disastrous.

There is also the risk that the target will notice the vulnerability that is being exploited and simply fix it. Many modern malwares, for example, act toward isolating a system from updates, as was seen with the Confikr worm (Bowden 2011, 54; Dhanjani, Rios, and Hardin 2009, 3189) before carrying out their ultimate end. By doing this, they seek to prohibit any actions that might either detect their presence or correct a vulnerability that they might be dependent on. If an attempt at coercion can be turned aside by simply updating a system to the most recent version, then it will most likely be found to be ineffective.

Fourth, effective coercion ultimately relies on the coercer possessing significantly greater military power than the target to have a chance at success (Pape 1996, 45). In land-, sea-, and air-based operations this superiority is needed to create the relative freedom of action that enables effective denial strategies. While there may be some disagreements over the finer points of relative power, a general consensus does exist over which countries are militarily stronger than others in conventional terms. However, as no true cyber competition has occurred with two attributable actors, no equivalent scale exists for computer-based capabilities. Moreover, a coercive strategy through networked infrastructure will only be effective against very highly developed countries. Given these facts, very few countries are susceptible to cyber coercion.

The last problem with cyber coercion qua Pape's limitations of denial is one of attribution. Even if an effective strategy is implemented and carried out to its fullest extent, it is wasted effort unless the target knows with certainty who is carrying out the actions and what demands they are making. When combined with the points listed earlier, a delicate situation comes into being: if a coercer acts too strongly, he risks his ability to maintain coercive pressure. However, if he acts too stealthily, he risks non-attribution and failure.

Analysis of Problems Posed by Limitations

While there does exist the possibility for a successful network-based coercion campaign, it is remote. Most literature focuses on coercive attempts against civilian populations for the good reason that that segment of the population is far more vulnerable to attacks of this type. While some targeted attacks could be used to contribute to a larger coercive campaign, most possible actions fall short in one of two areas.

First, actions effecting general infrastructure such as traffic control, oil and electricity distribution, or economic structures harm the civilian population disproportionately over the military. As Pape points out, military forces tend to have auxiliary capabilities to provide for most of their needs (Pape 1996, 75). This reduces the logistical tail that is vulnerable to attack. Furthermore, in times of scarce resources, militaries usually have priority access to what resources are available. This results in most actions victimizing the civilian population while having negligible effects on the military. As explained earlier, population-centered coercion is rarely effective.

Second, the problem of creating a reliable, persistent, and effective framework through which to continue coercion poses a significant challenge. Aside from the attribution challenge explained earlier, it is hard to think of a way that a computer problem could elicit devastation similar to a bomb without rendering the system that it located on inoperative or exposing itself in such a way that it is allowed to remain a threat. Though some examples exist of malware that is capable of reaching non-networked systems, these remain costly and time consuming to create and ultimately rely on bad implementation of security best practices (Falliereet al. 2011, 3).

This is not to say that computer operations could not be used to augment the efforts of a larger coercive effort. When used in this way, actions could be taken against targets of opportunity while a greater effort could be put into sabotaging critical components (Pape 1996, 71) and decreasing the efficiency of the overall manufacturing system. Though this is a costly and time-consuming procedure, limiting the target list to several facilities could allow teams enough time to conceivably hinder the production of needed military goods.

Further Limitations

While the lens of Pape's thinking can serve as a tool to evaluate network attack, other authors have tackled this topic in a more head-on fashion. Most significantly, Thomas Rid and Brandon Valeriano and Ryan Maness seat computer operations firmly within greater frameworks of international relations and war. Jason Healey also offers useful advice, drawing from a well of knowledge gained from studying incidents of cyber conflict dating back to the 1980s. Lastly, there is a huge body of technical knowledge that seems largely absent from academic policy writings, yet can add significant depth and texture to any discussion.

In *Cyber War Will Not Take Place*, Thomas Rid makes a compelling case that war as defined by Carl von Clausewitz is unlikely to be waged solely with computers. He also enumerates, based on his analysis, the three avenues that computer operations could potentially be useful. Finally, he also creates a continuum for classifying what he calls "cyber weapons."

Referencing Clausewitz, Rid focuses on the three qualities that separate war from simple violence or contention: war is violent, war is instrumental, and war is political (Rid 2013, 2). While cyber operations can easily fit the second and third criteria, true violence is difficult to create reliably. Though SCADA vulnerabilities can lead to destructive malfunctions and even possibly explosions, it is hard to consistently construct threats that have a serious chance of causing death or injury to civilian or military personnel (Rid 2013, 66).

Continuing to reference Clausewitz, Rid moves on to the structural aims of war, namely to disrupt trust between a population and its government and military (Rid 2013, 22). In normal circumstances, this trust is attacked through violence; as the population loses faith in its institutions they begin to lose trust in each other until either the state capitulates or order breaks down completely. Cyber attacks can—in theory—facilitate this lack of trust through non-violent means.

Rid gives three ways that this can happen: through espionage, through sabotage, and through subversion (Rid 2013, 10). Espionage erodes trust by showing that a government is incapable of protecting its citizens' digital assets. This is, as Rid points out, not only non-violent but also of questionable instrumentality as theft is a clandestine activity and likely would not be publicized (Rid 2013, 81). Sabotage is similarly hamstrung as a vector of war as it aims to disrupt the trust of groups in their equipment, as was seen in the Stuxnet attacks. Once the source of the sabotage is presented, or even the existence of sabotage, this trust is restored (Rid 2013, 32). This leaves subversion as the best avenue for a true "cyber war," though the least likely to be classified as such because any resulting contention or violence is likely to be seen as internal struggle instead of the result of malicious code (Rid 2013, 114).

Finally, Rid provides a useful continuum for classifying the tools of cyber conflict. On one side are weapons that are broadly effective yet produce minimal results. Denial of service attacks (DoS) and website vandalism fall in this category as they are effective to some degree on all Internet-connected devices yet cause little lasting damage. The continuum's other side are tools like Stuxnet, which are deeply impactful yet highly specific. These are the equivalent of a sniper's bullet that can cause massive amounts of damage yet must be tailored very specifically to a given target (Rid 2013, 35).

In contrast to Rid's forecasting, Valeriano and Maness attempt to empirically quantify what we already know about cyber conflict. Significantly, they approach the issue from the assumption that cyber conflict is a sphere of diplomacy rather than warfare, neatly sidestepping Rid's questions of the need for violence. From this vantage point, they see several interesting trends: first, that almost all cyber attacks are rooted in a pre-existing rivalry. Second, those attempting to use cyber weapons are very likely to be restrained in their use. Lastly, states will sometimes actively support cyber terrorism, though only in very specific situations.

The bedrock observation of Maness and Valeriano is that cyber contention stems from traditional interstate rivalries, similar to economic and military contention (Valeriano and Maness 2015, 8). This means that the process of attribution, usually held up as a key problem in cyber warfare, is simplified as the list of potential suspects is greatly reduced. Also, it signifies that the vast majority of conflicts will occur between neighbors, as they are more likely to be in contention with one another than countries with no shared borders. Moreover, the exceptions to this rule will be more significant and more constrained than non-neighbors.

Next, the nature of cyber conflict incentivizes restraint in its use. Because cyber tools are less predictable than conventional munitions, they are more likely to go awry in several ways: most significantly, they can be difficult to control, meaning that unintentional overreach is a possibility (Valeriano and Maness 2015, 4). Second, as cyber munitions are not expended when used, there is the possibility that victims or even third parties will reuse the tools for their own ends. This restraint will likely manifest itself in the use of cyber tools for primarily low-level actions, such as espionage, or to exploit obvious weaknesses (Valeriano and Maness 2015, 72).

Lastly, Valeriano and Maness claim that states have and will resort to cyber terrorism in certain situations. Primarily, state-sponsored cyber terrorism will allow less powerful nations to act with greater effect against more powerful foes. Second, states will resort to terrorism when they wish to distance themselves from their actions. Finally states will resort to terrorism when they want to quickly amplify their power for very simple purposes, as was seen in the Russian–Estonian War of 2007 (Valeriano and Maness 2015, 70). Interestingly, Valeriano and Maness do not seem confident that cyber terrorism can effect change.

Jason Healey's sweeping recap of conflict in the cyber arena, *A Fierce Domain*, covers a whole range of what could be termed "cyber attacks," between 1980 and 2012. While many of the attacks that he discusses are purely civilian in nature, the lessons learned from aggregation show that relatively little has changed in the past 35 years. Key among these lessons is the importance of public–private cooperation in computing crises, the nebulous nature of US cyber command and control, and that, in general, the more significant a cyber conflict is, the more similar it is to other conflicts.

From the beginning of cyber conflict, the importance of sharing of information between the public and private sectors has been crucial to both defense and recovery from attacks. This is seen as early as 1986's Lawrence Berkley Labs intrusions (Healey 2013, 2117) to as recently as the recovery from 2007's Estonian "cyber war" (Healey 2013, 1691). Similarly, in offense some states often employ or allow non-state actors to contribute to state-led efforts, as is seen in Healey's chart, Spectrum of State Responsibility (Healey 2013, 1218), and was also demonstrated in the 2007 Estonian event.

Contrasting this need for cooperation is the way in which the United States has handled the increasing militarization of cyber security. Healey quotes General Dusty Rhodes, former head of the 609th Information Warfare Squadron as saying that it was a great detriment to the cause of information security that all of the 609th's offensive operations remained classified, as well as many of their defensive actions (Healey 2013, 807). This is expounded upon by other statements made by other military commanders and policymakers (Healey 2013, 1126, 1327) indicating that many neglected cyber capabilities are due to their poor integration within the military structure. Put together, these sentiments point to a system that was and largely still is isolated from much of the day-to-day operations of the groups that it claims to protect.

Lastly, similar to Valeriano and Maness, Healey makes the argument that cyber conflicts behave more similarly to non-cyber crises as they grow in significance, with one exception. That exception, the increased presence and ability of non-state actors, is squarely at odds with arguments made by Valeriano and Maness (Healey 2013, 494). This differentiation is important, as it substantially broadens the field of potential attackers, introduces more variance in how they act, and complicates attribution.

Technical Writings

While many policymakers and thinkers are familiar with the sources cited above, there is another category of sources that are rarely referenced. There is a large and ever-growing trove of books, blogs, and media published both formally and informally that shows the conflict over security from the tactical side rather than the political. While much of this information is of little value to decision makers, there are certain fundamentals that can give those at the strategic and political levels of decision-making valuable insights.

First, there are the core goals of security. According to Harris, an expert on information security, the goal of a computer security is to maintain data in a way that it is always available, accurate, and confidential (Harris 2012, 1212). At first glance, this maps very closely to Rid's sabotage, subversion, and espionage, as each attack targets its respective value (sabotage attacks availability, subversion targets accuracy, and espionage targets confidentiality). Still, as Harris goes on to point out most businesses (and governments) do not exist to be secure, that is security is a secondary goal that has no value if the company is not successful in its primary endeavor. Contrary to kinetic warfare where a state by definition must have a monopoly over force within its borders, computer security will always be less important than physical security and day-to-day government operations.

Closely tied to these goals are the concepts of risk, threat, and vulnerability (Figure 1). While these terms are used in both the kinetic and computer arenas, in computer security, these words have very specific meanings: a threat is a possible danger. A threat agent is something that actually uses a threat to cause damage, assuming that vulnerability can be found. Risk is the probability that one's assets take damage from a threat agent given once exposure and safeguards (Harris 2012, 1312)

This model warrants a moment's consideration, as most of the hyperbole that Rid, Valeriano and Maness, and Healey frequently reference can be seen in this model. In the arguments of thinkers like Richard Clarke and Winn Schwartau, both noted for their contributions to information security policy, there are effectively an infinite number of threats and vulnerabilities meaning that there is a near infinite risk. This has clearly not been the case as observed by the authors profiled in the previous section and is due largely to difficulty of constructing treat agents that can act in concert with a states' wishes while limiting the probability of blowback.

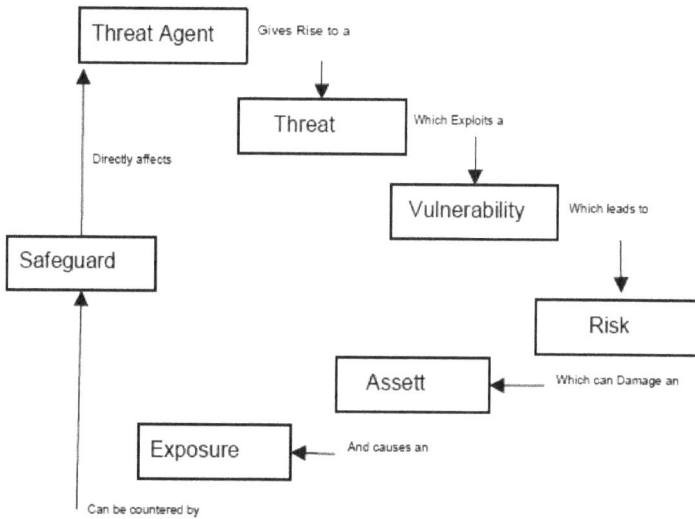

Figure 1: Relationships of Different Security Concepts (Shon 2012, 1312)

Next is the concept of defense-in-depth, wherein layers of protective measures are used to provide overlapping means of security. According to Harris, these layers can each have one of six functions (Harris 2012, 1343) as follows.

Deterrent	Discourages a potential attacker
Preventive	Intended to avoid an accident
Corrective	Fixes a component/system after an incident
Recovery	Intended to bring environment back to normal
Detective	Watches a system's activities for signs of an incident
Compensating	Provides an alternate measure of control

While not all of these functions can realistically scale up to a strategic or political level, it is very clear that some of these have been favored above others in the discussions on security. For example, Valeriano and Maness extensively discuss the lack of utility of a deterrent strategy and the NSA's mandate to secure the American military space is very akin to a strategic-level detective function. Still, rather than focusing on preventative measures as the only solution, other options such as compensation and correction might well have a place in a strategic computer security solution.

Further Analysis

The various insights of the aforementioned authors paint a much more complete picture of cyber conflict as it exists today. Rid's integration of cyber war into the Clausewitzian understanding of war is significant, though by dropping the traditional requirement of violence, more understanding can be gained. Similarly,

Valeriano and Maness' framing of cyber conflict within the greater international system yields great possibility for moving thought forward on this topic.

Rid's assertion that trust is key in cyber attacks is crucial to understanding the landscape; however, there are more functions that attack trust than just espionage, sabotage, and subversion. An additional three "hybrid attacks" are conceivable, each a combination of two basic types (Figure 2). These are insurgency, transparency, and APT (advanced persistent threat).

APT is a term that used to be reserved for high-level state threats, but is now used to denote any threat that has the long-term capability to enter a computer system at will and take information. APT is usually achieved by sabotaging the computer's security system crippling its abilities to detect the intrusion and subsequently exfiltrate information. This has been seen in a number of incidents—usually attributed to the Chinese state—including the Moonlight Maze and Night Dragon attacks (Healey 2013, 1138, 1611).

Insurgency, much like its kinetic counterpart, is a combination of subversion and sabotage. This type of attack is what Valeriano and Maness refer to as state-sponsored cyber-terrorism. In these incidents, non-state forces are coerced into acting on the state's behalf to publicly sabotage a target of the state's choosing, undermining trust in the state. Examples of cyber insurgency are the 2007 Russian–Estonian conflict and the computer component of 2008's Russian–Georgian War.

Transparency is arguably the most powerful attack methodology, a combination of espionage and subversion. Though the results of this vector are rarely considered a cyber incident, well-timed revelations of stolen information like the Edward Snowden leaks or WikiLeaks can have a huge subversive effect on a population.

All three of these hybrid attack methodologies are unique to their fundamental counterparts in scope. APT is greater than simple espionage in that it creates a paranoia that undercuts trust more thoroughly once it is detected and exfiltrates more information while it is being used. Similarly, transparency is more effective than simple espionage because it is noticed more and can undercut not only institutional trust but also faith in institutional motives. Lastly, infiltration can create an ad hoc strategic weapon capable of surpassing the tactical capabilities of most cyber tools.

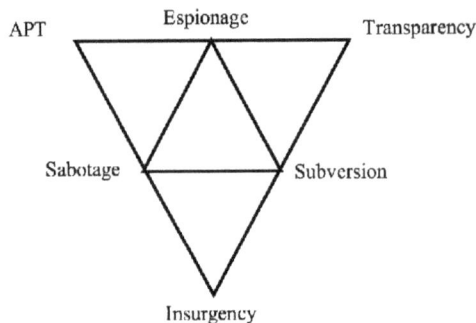

Figure 2: A Riddian Triad Modified with Hybrid Attack Methods

Worth noting in the examples above is the presence of non-state actors. Healey writes that as cyber crises become more significant, they become more like traditional crises save the greater number of non-state actors. This is in contention with Valeriano and Maness (2015, 165), who claim that non-state actors have little effect on states in a cyber conflict other than that they may be co-opted into a state's official plans. This is an unrealistic expectation for several reasons.

First, if the true aim of an attack is to damage a population's trust in its institutions, it stands to reason that portions of a population will become involved in the conflict if the barriers to entry are low enough. This is related to Pape's "rally around the flag," and is similar to resistance movements around the world. The Internet's low entry criteria and huge potential for individual anonymity create the perfect situation for individual involvement.

Second, as the Estonia–Russia conflict of 2007 shows, in times of extreme crisis, it is civilians, not state forces that are available to assist (Healey 2013, 1693). The reasons for this are twofold: primarily, it is because the Internet is run by nongovernmental groups and these are the groups with the expertise to aid in large-scale restructuring of network infrastructure. Additionally, because state assets are many times bound in nebulous command structures that prioritize secrecy, they are unable to help directly. This non-state, ad-hoc cooperation was also seen in the public response to the Windows Confikr worm (Bowden 2011), as well in 1986's Lawrence Berkley Labs (Cookoo's Egg) intrusions (Healey 2013, 2125).

Lastly, as the Internet and its users mature, non-state actors' abilities are constantly growing. Far from the website vandalism and DDoS attacks of the early 2000s, individuals, such as the social activist "The Jester", are able to cause significant real damage by themselves. When individuals with these skills lend or sell them to groups with political agendas, the result is semisophisticated incidents like 2012's Shamoon virus which targeted Saudi Aramco computers (Rid 2013, 56). Also, as the 2015 breakup of Italy's Hacking Team shows, non-state groups are actively developing a sophisticated arsenal of digital tools (Security Week 2015) that are being used by states.

While the presence of these non-state entities does complicate Valeriano and Maness' ease of attribution, it does not create undue confusion. Most of these non-state groups are interested primarily in crime and will only become involved in political events when they are tapped by their respective states (Carr 2009, 28). Other groups, like those that administer and run the Internet, have little interest in causing unrest and will only become involved in an incident to mitigate and diagnose problems.

These groups can, however, be classified in a way that can give clue to their intentions (Figure 3). When classified as either legal or illegal and further subdivided by level of organization a pattern emerges

	Organized	Illegal
Legal	• Infrastructure groups (IETF, ICANN, W3C) • Antivirus companies • University researchers • Professional groups (SANS)	• Working groups (NSC-SEC, Confikr Working Group) • Individual researchers
Individual / Ad Hoc	• Individual hackers • "Hacktivists" • Disgruntled insiders	• Individual hackers • "Hacktivists" • Disgruntled insiders

Figure 3: Types of Non-State Actors in Cyber Events and Examples

In general, each quadrant has common goals. Entities in the top left quadrant (Legal, Organized), have a vested interest in maintaining order online and understanding and mitigating systemic threats. While they are very unlikely to instigate problems, they are usually in the forefront of solving most major problems. The top right square (Legal, Individual/Ad Hoc) contains many of those that actually solve systemic crises. A common model, as seen in the reaction to the Estonian crisis and the Confikr virus, is for individuals associated with the groups in the first quadrant to come together to form and execute a solution.

The bottom row contains the groups that are likely to have a part in instigating crises, though only in well-defined contexts. The bottom left quadrant (Illegal, Organized) is traditionally the domain of organized crime groups, such as the infamous Russian Business Group. Though usually interested in traditional criminal enterprises, there is evidence that these groups have engaged in political activities with state sponsorship. Similarly, online wings of terrorist groups are an emerging phenomenon, but, thus far, organized activities have been limited to propaganda and local activities.

These groups' capabilities can be highly sophisticated and targeted, as seen in the 2013 intrusion on the US shopping chain Target and The Cutting Sword of Justice's re-weaponization of the Wiper malware (CNET 2012). Still, most of these groups' activities are less spectacular and usually comprise identity theft and website defacement.

Lastly, the bottom-right corner (Illegal, Individual/Ad Hoc) is the realm of so-called "black hats," (malicious individuals) and hacktivists. These are groups and individuals usually focused on short-term goals and causes. While they can be technologically proficient, more often than not, they use tools that fall on the lower end of Rid's continuum (broadly targeted and lightly damaging). There is no evidence of these groups creating strategic-level incidents without state support.

The last entry in this quadrant, the disgruntled insider has proved to be the most significant cyber foe of states (Andress and Winterfeld 2011, 1028). This is the group that individuals like Edward Snowden and Chelsea Manning belong to. Their methods are rarely sophisticated, though their access means that they have little need of sophisticated methods.

To return to Rid's Clausewitian argument, what usually separates malicious state actors from non-state ones is not sophistication but scale. While many of these groups are quite technologically able, they have not yet moved beyond what would be termed an operational level in traditional military terms. All cyber weapons are tactical, as is pointed out by Rid (2013, 35) and they have shown themselves capable of creating focused campaigns to attack a given target from multiple angles. What is yet to be seen is these groups mounting a true strategic campaign, such as an attack across a whole industry or geographic area.

This is likely for several reasons: first, being interested in profit alone, they have little incentive to invest substantial resources in difficult targets so long as easier ones exist. Second, the range of vulnerabilities needed to threaten multiple systems and network architectures is substantially greater than those needed to threaten one.

Businesses, as Harris explains, exist to make money, not to be secure. This leads to a situation wherein there will always be "easy targets" due to competing priorities within a company and industry as a whole. This same logic, incidentally, also applies to state groups acting under restraint as described by Valeriano and Maness: so long as targets exist that are easily attacked with little chance of bleeding into other sectors, there is little reason to devote the substantial resources needed to develop a Stuxnet-like threat (2015, 63). Overspill is of concern due to unintended consequences that might accompany losing control of a tool. Concern for this overreach can be seen in several tools: Confikr contained a test wherein if a computer was using a Ukrainian keyboard it would not be effected, likely for legal reasons (Bowden 2011, 56). Similarly, Sutxnet, the poster child of high-end malware, was carefully written to only effect the very particular combinations of hardware and software that were used in a certain Iranian nuclear refinery.

Second, as the Stuxnet dossier shows, creating highly targeted, hard hitting software is difficult. Sophisticated though it was, Stuxnet was only a tactical tool. If one compares it to its brethren in the Olympic Games campaign, it quickly becomes apparent that Rid's tradeoffs between complexity and range are very real. The ability to create a series of these tools to be used in coordination required not one but at least four separate tools, each with its own purposes. To return to the air power analogies that were made earlier in this paper, to create a one-size-fits-all cyber weapon would be similar to creating a single airplane that could simultaneously act in all the roles needed by a modern air force.

As Harris states, defense-in-depth is the standard when protecting digital assets. In general, the more valuable the target, the greater number of layers of defense it utilizes. While each layer may have one or multiple vulnerabilities, finding the correct threats to exploit these vulnerabilities in sequence is time consuming and difficult, especially if any failed attempts will result in patches to the system, thus negating previous work. Moreover, there are communities of professionals in place that frequently communicate known vulnerabilities, meaning that a failed attempt on one target might result in other targets becoming aware of their vulnerabilities.

Targets can be classified into five tiers, numbered one to five, with an additional level (numbered zero) for specific cases. These tiers are clusters of traits that should coalesce given a network's assets, contents, and security goals and tolerances. While they are not hard-edged cases, they are useful when thinking about a network or company's security stance.

Type one targets are typical of military installations. Given their highly secret nature and zero tolerance for breaches, they are highly controlled and have very complex security protocols that control both digital and physical access (NAVFAC 2015). Typically, they are secured beyond a level necessitated by normal compliance standards and are quick to react to any perceived threat. Due to their nature, however, they are slow to disclose any known vulnerabilities, meaning that attacks made on these systems can possibly be repeated elsewhere against non-military targets.

Tier two targets are less complex but still in compliance with a rigid set of industry standards. A typical type two target is a financial institution, multinational corporation, or non-military government facility. Their need to be secure is balanced by their need to be accessible to a wide number of users, creating inherent tradeoffs in security versus usability. While security is a priority for these groups, often times there is an element of calculated risk, balancing money spent on security against the costs associated with being exploited. They can be slow or fast to react to threats, with private sector entities tending to react faster due to the need to be seen as secure. If exploited, they are typically quick to disclose the attack.

The third type of target is typical of a business of medium size. It is generally in compliance with industry standards, though these may be allowed to slip between evaluation periods. These industry standards, like PCI (for taking credit cards), are usually the extent of security procedures. If they are attacked, they may be less quick to react and will only disclose the attack if it is deemed economically sound, especially if they are not in an industry that is especially security conscious.

Fourth is the level of security seen in most homes and small businesses. There is little, if any regulated security structures, and most of these are protocol driven and standardized. As a group, type four targets are slow to react to vulnerabilities and are often unaware of their risk. If an attack or vulnerability is discovered, it is likely reported quickly through professional groups though updates to mitigate the vulnerabilities are often slow to be applied.

The last level, zero, is reserved for hardware and embedded systems. These are typical of consumer level "Internet of Things," devices, though other devices like rolling-code garage doors (the most common type of remotely operated door) and Bluetooth devices also fall into this category. If vulnerability is discovered, it is often hard or impossible to mitigate without replacing hardware.

These levels are, as stated before, not clear-cut distinctions but rather common clusters of traits based on priorities. They become significant in state-level security because they offer a series of tradeoffs that a potential attacker or defender must consider. On one hand, the simplest targets are easy to attack and control but are of limited instrumentality and clearly within the civilian sphere, meaning that blowback will likely be significant. To balance that, the more instrumental targets (like military systems) are more difficult to attack and also less likely to be disclosed publicly if successful.

The best target for an attacker is the one that is likely to be disclosed publically but does not directly affect the population at large and must balance the ability to rapidly change with the ability to be accessible to a large number of people. This means that type two systems that do not directly affect the public are the ideal target to undermine trust in institutions. Because they are quick to disclose attacks and slow to be able to change, the likelihood of creating great effects is significant.

Still, within the past year, there have been two attacks that fit this description, one on the US Office of Personnel Management and another one on the American offices of Sony Pictures. Neither, however, seems to have gained the traction that would be needed to be deemed effective.

Conclusion

While the term "cyber warfare," is used often, it is difficult to foresee a true cyberwar. Though network-based attacks are capable of producing some impact on physical systems, these are mostly one-off in nature and require a significant amount of time and planning per attack, making them an unlikely choice as a primary coercive measure. Similarly, though much time and effort has been put into planning for a limitless cyber attack on the US population, there is evidence that this type of attack will have little chance of success. The most likely role for cyber attacks in the near future will likely be variations on how they are used today: espionage, sabotage, and subversion. Still, there are models that can be used to classify targets, attackers, their tools, and their aims. By using these frameworks we can get a better understanding of the computer battlefield. In the near future, analytic value will come from seeing if and how these frameworks continue to be relevant.

References

Andress, Jason, and Steve Winterfeld. 2011. *Cyber Warfare: Techniques, Tactics and Tools for Security Practitioners*. Kindle Edition. New York: Syngress Press.

Bentek Systems. 2012. "Internet and Web SCADA." http://www.scadalink.com/support/web-based-scada.html (accessed September 14, 2015).

Bowden, Mark. 2011. *Worm: The First Digital World War. Kindle Edition*. New York: Atlantic Monthly Press.

Bradbeer, Thomas G. 2004. "Battle of Air Supremacy Over the Somme: 1 June–30 November 1916." MS Thesis, US Army Command and General Staff College.

Brenner, Joel. 2011. *America the Vulnerable: Inside the New Threat Matrix of Digital Espionage, Crime, and Warfare*. Kindle Edition. New York, New York: The Penguin Press.

Carr, Jeffery. 2009. *Inside Cyber Warfare: Mapping the Cyber Underworld*. Kindle Edition. Boston, Massachusetts:O'Riley.

CNET. 2012. "A Who's Who of Mideast-Targeted Malware." http://www.cnet.com/news/a-whos-who-of-mideast-targeted-malware/ (accessed September 14, 2015).

Dhanjani, Nitesh, Billy Rios, and Brett Hardin. 2009. *Hacking: The Next Generation*. Kindle Edition. Boston, Massachusetts:O'Riley.

Falliere, Nicolas, Liam O. Murchu, and Eric Chien. 2011. "W32.Stuxnet Dossier." http://www.symantec.com/content/en/us/enterprise/media/security_response/whitepapersw32_stuxnet_dossier.pdf

Ferrari, Dino, Trans. 1942. *Giulio Douhet Command of the Air*. New York: Coward McCann.

Harris, Shon. 2012. *CISSP All-in-One Exam Guide*, Sixth Edition, Kindle Edition. New York, New York:McGraw-Hill Education.

Healey, Jason. 2013. *A Fierce Domain: Conflict in Cyberspace, 1986 to 2012*. Kindle Edition. Vienna, Virginia:Cyber Conflict Studies Association.

Pape, Robert A. 1996. *Bombing to Win: Air Power and Coercion in War*. Ithica, New York: Cornell University Press.

NAVFAC. "Physical Security of Sensitive Compartmented Information Facilities." https://www.wbdg.org/pdfs/dod_at/navfac_scif_ho.pdf (accessed September 14, 2015).

Rid, Thomas. 2013. *Cyber War Will Not Take Place*. Kindle Edition. New York: Oxford University Press.

Security Week. "Zero Day Exploits Released in Hacking Team Leak." http://www.securityweek.com/zero-day-exploits-leaked-hacking-team-breach (accessed September 14, 2015).

Valeriano, Brandon, and Ryan C. Maness. 2015. *Cyber War versus Cyber Realities: Cyber Conflict in the International System*. Kindle Edition. New York: Oxford University Press.

Review of *500 Days: Secrets and Lies in the Terror Wars*

Kurt Eichenwald (2012). *500 Days: Secrets and Lies in the Terror Wars*. New York: Touchstone Books. pp. XXX.$30.

Arguably *500 Days: Secrets and Lies in the Terror Wars* may be the most important book to come out of not only the current Global War on Terror, but perhaps into the future. Eichenwald's has boldly staked out a position that is only perhaps the fringes of the two sides of the political spectrum can truly rail against. What we have is a carefully detailed exposition of what went on in the Bush Administration and the United States Government shortly before the attacks of September 11, 2001 and subsequent policy decisions. It is my conjecture that many of the actions undertaken by this administration would have been repeated in large part by any other at that moment in time—a question that Eichenwald never once raises but should have. I think to be generous, some of the folks in the book have made decisions they thought were in the nation's best interests.

Eichenwald's book is truly panoramic and global in its sweep. The reader is treated to the critical, and not so critical events spanning from Syria, Afghanistan, Bali to the Anthrax letters in DC. The scope of Eichenwald's book is indeed ambitious, and as one who worked on aspects at different levels and was affected by the actions he describes, the tale and narrative he weaves is both compelling and morbidly fascinating. When one reads early on that John Ashcroft, the Attorney General of the United States, didn't even include terrorism as one of his top priorities, you simply have to ponder what the train of thinking was to reach that conclusion, after the USS Cole less than a year earlier. Or comments like the FBI Special Supervisory Agent Michael Maltbie who denied the request for a search warrant of the 911 hijackers, indicating the malaise and slothful indifference to thinking outside the box was deep seated in the Federal bureaucracy.

Giving "intelligence" from Syria the same validity and credence as intelligence produced by the American and Western Intelligence Communities would allow us to be seduced by fabrications of those who were telling their Syrian torturers what they thought they wanted to hear. It boggles the mind that no one asked to sit in on one of these interrogation sessions. Syria, Egypt, and Saudi Arabia were notorious for the human rights violations in their penal system—how did no one make the logical jump and assume that interrogations of suspected terrorists would go yet further south than that?

There are some characters who come off quite poorly in the book. Perhaps the worst of the worst is John Yoo, who seemed to think that he could redefine the established law of the land. George Tenet comes off poorly, a bureaucrat trying to regain credibility after failing to protect the nation. Tenet aggressively pursued waterboarding at Guantanamo Bay, spearheaded charitably by what one might label a crackpot psychologist. Interrogations went from brutal to more than illegal,

doi: 10.18278/gsis.1.2.6

repeatedly slamming detainees into the plywood walls, in the name of truth seeking. Even better, try and keep track of the numbers as they grow—the final count reaches 183 times on one individual.

What the book does do is paint a picture in narrative form of much of what I had known at the classified level, but in a manner that encompasses the totality of the subject. The fight over waterboarding in retrospect could not have been any more mishandled than it was by supposedly constitutional lawyers. What makes the reader cringe while reading the sections on water boarding is not the technique per se, but the fact that it generally is shown to be seldom effective. In fact, what we had was a group of people who simply decided to "Cowboy Up" on how interrogations would be conducted. In fact it is easy to see this type of thinking and distinct lack of understanding of the value of real interrogations that leads to real intelligence ends up in the sewer of Abu Grab?

But Eichenwald, for all the good stuff stuff, perhaps, missed some real obvious things. With but a little homework, he would have discovered that the U.S. ARMY Reserves have many professional interrogators. Had he then used that to ask why the CIA chose to go down the dark path they did with a crackpot, his story would have been immeasurably strengthened. Nor does the author give the Manchester Manual the proper amount of analysis, instead consigning it conveniently to an appendix, where most readers will simply ignore it—but shouldn't.

If there is but one book Americans should read on the events post 9/11, 500 Days is the one. It is the benchmark for books to be measured against in terms of in-depth and relatively unbiased reporting. It is compelling and simply very hard to put down. It is easy to see a linear path of the adoption of these techniques to believing in the necessity of the war in Iraq.

Robert Smith

Review of *Propaganda and Intelligence in the Cold War: The NATO Information Service*

Linda Risso (2014). *Propaganda and Intelligence in the Cold War: The NATO Information Service*. London: Routledge.

In her analysis of propaganda during the Cold War, Linda Risso argues that the NATO Information Service (NATIS) conducted a robust propaganda campaign despite member states' conflicting interests. According to Riso, NATIS and Western intelligence services formed a symbiotic relationship; the spy agencies provided intelligence to aid the propaganda campaign and NATIS returned the favor by furnishing information. To back this thesis, the author examined documents from the NATO archives and conducted interviews with key policymakers. Overall, Risso's analysis is a solid contribution to the literature on multilateral cooperation and propaganda, although the policy implications are less explicit.

The book is separated into two sections with the first half examining the formation of NATIS at the beginning of the Cold War. Throughout this section, Risso pays particular attention to how outside events affected NATO's propaganda campaign. For example, she details how Josef Stalin's death and the conflict in Korea led to an expansion of NATIS' propaganda efforts. These details help the reader understand how NATO's propaganda efforts developed while at the same time filling a gap in the intelligence literature on how propaganda agencies worked together during the Cold War. The proceeding chapters detail how the turbulence of the 1960s led to a greater emphasis on targeting propaganda campaigns towards younger generations and how the relationship between NATIS and the media evolved during the 1980s.

Readers will notice immediately that *Propaganda and Intelligence in the Cold War* is remarkable in its attention to detail. Risso does an excellent job providing context while keeping the focus on NATIS. Students of NATO history and propaganda will also be satisfied with the attention to detail and primary source material. However, those looking for a more explicit tie to contemporary policy might leave with some unanswered questions. For example, given NATIS' history what are the implications for current propaganda agencies? Would the lessons of NATIS hold true for similar international organizations not engaged in propaganda operations? These policy-relevant questions are not addressed except for a few paragraphs in the introductory and concluding chapters.

Another area that would have been interesting to draw out further is the author's most interesting claim: the reciprocal relationship between intelligence and propaganda efforts. Although there is a description of how NATIS worked with intelligence agencies broadly, Risso spends little time explicitly exploring the relationship beyond the discussion in Chapter 2. A longer explanation would have been interesting given the importance of this claim, not only for the book, but for the broader intelligence studies literature.

doi: 10.18278/gsis.1.2.7

The second half of this book is a description of the various policies used by NATIS to influence public opinion. These include NATO films and exhibitions, engagement with opinion leaders in the intelligentsia, and work with voluntary organizations. This is a clear contribution to the literature on Cold War propaganda because it suggests that over time the scope of NATIS' efforts broadened to include a wider portion of the public. Still, it would be interesting to learn more about the effectiveness of these activities, but this is a difficult, if not impossible task as the author notes (pp. 253–254).

While this book is light on policy recommendations implications, it is a solid contribution to the literature. Historians will be pleased with the author's attention to historical detail and use of previously unexplored NATO documents and those interested in international cooperation will find an excellent example of how states can work together in peace and crises.

Stephen Coulthart
National Security Studies Institute, University of Texas, El Paso, Texas

Review of *An International History of the Cuban Missile Crisis*

David Gioe, Len Scott, and Christopher Andrew (2014). *An International History of the Cuban Missile Crisis*. London: Routledge. ISBN: 978-0-415-73217-8 (hbk). ISBN: 978-1-315-81727-9 (ebk). 307 pages

>   *An International History of the Cuban Missile Crisis* (Gioe et al. 2014) is a compilation of various independent works on the global perspectives of the 1962 Cuban missile crisis. The editors note that the various pieces focus on three key areas, including the importance of memory, intelligence achievements and failings, and the risks of nuclear war (Gioe et al. 2014).

   Many of the pieces in this compilation focus on the gaps between personally recorded historical perspectives and information widely available in pre-existing literature on the history of the Cuban missile crisis. For example, Andrew and Catterall portray the importance of public perception and media during the crisis (Andrew 2014, 9–24; Catterall 2014, 72–98). The use personal accounts during the crisis by both leadership and common civilians give testament to the images and perceptions not otherwise noted in common sources on the crisis. The analyses of personal accounts provide valuable comparative material for students in political science and international relations studying the differences between public and leadership attitudes during the Cuban missile crisis. Various pieces also provide more insight into the various processes by which policy decisions were made during the crisis. For example Munton's piece titled the *Fourth Question* focuses on considerations behind John F. Kennedy's decision to offer up the Jupiter missiles in Turkey (Munton 2014, 258–278). Furthermore, the personal historical accounts as well as the accounts of media coverage on the crisis (Seaton and Hughes 2014, 43–71) serve to initiate discussion on the similarities and differences between the U.S. and British reactions to the imminent threat of nuclear war in 1962 with those of today by both civilian and political figures. Unfortunately, the literature on memory does not address how the U.S. population could react today to an equivalent threat of nuclear war given different views, threat perceptions, and the long forgotten memories of the destruction of the nuclear bombs unleashed during World War II. Thus, although substantive in the ability to add to the pre-existing literature on the perceptions and images of the Cuban missile crisis of 1962, the section on memory falls short to relate how the memory of the 1962 Cuban missile crisis informs how international conflicts are remembered today or how similar conflicts may be remembered in the future.

   The accounts of intelligence achievements and failures during the Cuban missile crisis also add to the existing literature, yet also fall short on extrapolating how lessons learned impact intelligence practices today. The pieces on intelligence activity during the crisis read more to the tune of a historical narrative of which there is already an abundance of on the Cuban missile crisis. For example, Goodman's piece

doi: 10.18278/gsis.1.2.8

titled the *Joint Intelligence Committee and the Cuban missile crisis* (Goodman 2014, 99–105) and Peterson's piece titled *A trial by fire* (Peterson 2014, 106–134) provided additional historical perspectives on the roles of the Joint Intelligence Committee (JIC) and the emergence of the DIA but do not deeply discuss the impacts of the crisis on the JIC or the Defense Intelligence Agency (DIA) today. Once again, the literature incorporated into this book regarding intelligence activity adds to further historical narratives of the Cuban missile crisis, yet does not discuss how or why many of the same perception and image problems, as well as organizational problems continued, or play into how the U.S intelligence community approaches new threats, collects and analyzes intelligence, works with ally intelligence services, or creates actionable intelligence today. The various works presented in this compilation on the intelligence community are thus best read in conjunction with more formal works on critical thinking, political psychology, and intelligence community history. Recommended additional readings for the intelligence pieces found in this compilation might include Cottam et al.'s (2010) *Introduction to Political Psychology*, Cottam's (1994) *Images and Intervention U.S Policies in Latin America*, and Jeffrey T. Richelson's (1997) *A Century of Spies Intelligence in the Twentieth Century*.

    In regards to the topic of weapons of mass destruction, this compilation focuses more on political implications and perceptions and less on lessons learned and future considerations. Although none of the pieces were found to directly speak to the issue of how Weapons of Mass Destruction (WMD) affect policy and intelligence operations, the topic is primarily present in recounts of individual historical perspectives and the worries of various international bodies such as the UN and third parties such as Australia and Italy. For example, Scott's piece titled *Intelligence and the risk of nuclear war* (Scott 2014, 25–42) focuses on the perception and attitudes toward nuclear war as well as leadership profiles, and less on the interpretation of intelligence data or practices in regards to a nuclear crisis. The literature focusing on intelligence provides little insight regarding the implications of WMD policy today, such as the lack of international consensus on what now constitutes a WMD. What this book lacks is the ability to connect how the lessons learned from the Cuban missile crisis have affected policy and intelligence operations today. For example, although Kent and Naumkim (2014) address how Russia perceives and remembers the Cuban missile crisis today, no insight is given into how the relationship that was forged during the Cold War between Russia and Cuba (and further strengthened by the Cuban missile crisis) is currently impacted by recent developments regarding the United States lifting the Cuban embargo today. These types of topics are of extreme interest to intelligence professionals and students today.

    Overall, this compilation best supplements pre-existing literature on the Cuban missile crisis, but does not add new insight into current Cuban–International or Cuban–U.S affairs. For those personally interested in behind the scenes political perceptions and the various reactions of the U.S. and British public to the threat of nuclear war; this book provides good source material and rare insights into personal reactions to the crisis. For students of political science and international studies this book serves as an adequate compilation of additional historical perspectives on the inner workings of policy and international negotiation during the Cuban missile crisis. For students in intelligence studies, this book is best used only as a source for specific pieces on intelligence community history during the Cuban missile crisis as it focuses heavily on history and less on lessons learned or the intimate intricacies of the various intelligence disciplines used during the crisis to collect and analyze data. Overall, this book compiles a variety of interesting pieces which help further understand the inner workings and underpinnings of the Cuban missile crisis, yet it does not offer the necessary discussions on future policy and intelligence considerations during WMD threats which would have distinguished this book from the pre-existing literature on the Cuban missile crisis.

Briguette Carstensen
Honors Graduate,
American Military University's Master of Intelligence Studies and Analysis Program,
Charles Town, West Virginia

Review of *After the Sheikhs: The Coming Collapse of the Gulf Monarchies*

Christopher M. Davidson (2013). *After the Sheikhs: The Coming Collapse of the Gulf Monarchies.* London: Hurst & Company. ISBN: 978-1-84-904189-8. 300 pages.$34.95.

As they say, one should not judge a book by its cover. If one were to read this book without its cover and preface, one would come away convinced that the Gulf monarchies are facing serious challenges to their rule. Inside the book, from the introduction to the index, Davidson uses competent archival and interview research to document the internal and external pressures on the six Gulf monarchies and to draw relevant implications. Other than this, however, the book's analytical competence is questionable. Despite this, or perhaps because of it, this book should be read by anyone interested in Arabian Gulf studies.

Even if one should not judge a book by its cover, the picture on the cover of this book truly is worth a thousand words. There, the faces of the six Gulf monarchs are emblazoned on dominoes, teetering on the brink of collapse. The implicit message is made explicit in the preface, when Davidson unabashedly predicts that "most of these regimes—at least in their present form—will be gone *within the next two to five years*" (vii, emphasis in original). Since he made this prediction in 2012, it means that at least four of the six Gulf monarchies will fall between 2014 and 2017. While this prediction appears to be inaccurate, what is most damning to Davidson's argument is that he makes no attempt at all to link his theoretical or empirical analysis to this prediction. From the introduction to the index, there is no obvious mention of this 2–5 year prediction, except for the title of the sixth chapter, "The Coming Collapse." This startling analytical oversight—bold prediction decoupled from evidence—is a critical weakness of the book and frames the debate over the book not on the evidence and argument, but on the flimsy prediction.

There are other analytical shortfalls, as well. Davidson makes no comparisons to countries that did experience the kind of change that his prediction would entail. In fact, I was in Egypt on the eve of the January 25 revolution, and in Palestine on the eve of the al-Aqsa Intifada; the general tension and anger at the status quo were palpable there, which stands in stark contrast to the comparatively placid state of politics when I arrived in the UAE, sometime after the Arab Spring had begun. In addition, Davidson's analysis suffers from omitted variable bias; the strength and loyalty of the security services plays no real role in his argument. Instead, he assumes that the "coming collapse" is a function of external and internal pressures on the traditional Gulf monarchies alone. Had he taken the strength and loyalty of security forces into account, he likely would not have made such an ill-advised and anemic prediction about the fate of the Gulf monarchies.

The question, then, is whether the book should be read at all. From an academic perspective, the answer is an unqualified "yes"—no book is without

doi: 10.18278/gsis.1.2.9

flaws, and this is an opportunity to challenge Davidson on the interpretation of his evidence. In particular, it is important to ask, philosophically, whether a stiff response to opposition in the short term, followed by diffuse concessions in the longer term, constitutes a greater good than an immediate and destabilizing leap into democracy. This is an important question, and one that Davidson merely leaves implicit, focused as he is on the imperiled state of Western-style liberal activism in the Gulf, seemingly unable to see the larger issues at stake. In sum, *After the Sheikhs* is a book that is at least as insightful for its failings as for the evidence it presents, and it is always worth having an academic discussion about that.

Nathan W. Toronto
UAE National Defense College, Abu Dhabi, United Arab Emirates

Review of *The Rise of Islamic State: ISIS and the New Sunni Revolution; The Islamic State: A Brief Introduction; and The ISIS Apocalypse: The History, Strategy and Doomsday Vision of the Islamic State:*

Deconstructing the Islamic State

Cockburn, Patrick. *The Rise of Islamic State: ISIS and the New Sunni Revolution.* Brooklyn: Verso, 2015. ISBN 978-1-78478-040-1. pp. ix–xx, 1–161; index, pp. 165–172.

Lister, Charles R. *The Islamic State: A Brief Introduction.* Washington, DC: Brookings Institution Press, 2015. ISBN 978-0-8157-2667-8. pp. vii–xviii, 1–86; notes, pp. 87–101, index, pp. 103–110

McCants, William. *The ISIS Apocalypse: The History, Strategy and Doomsday Vision of the Islamic State.* New York: St. Martin's Press, 2015. ISBN 978-1-250-08090-5. pp. ix–xi, 1–181; notes, pp. 183–232; index, pp. 233–242.

Since the proclamation of the Islamic State in June 2014, scholars, government officials, and journalists, along with other observers, have struggled to understand the nature of this organization and to explain its rapid pattern of successes. The swift rise of the Islamic State, the capture of Mosul, and the announcement of a worldwide caliphate in the early summer of 2014 shocked the global community, the West in particular. Pledges of support from dozens of jihadist groups soon followed. By 2015, ISIS was claiming responsibility for or inspiring terrorist attacks around the world. The ability of ISIS to utilize social media to publicize its often brutal actions and to inspire or recruit followers has proved to be particularly troubling.

But what exactly is the Islamic State? Is it a military and political insurgency focused on redrawing the borders of the Middle East as a preliminary step toward fulfilling its goal of creating a global caliphate and establishing its authority over the world's Muslims? Is it a terrorist organization? Is it both? These and other questions are addressed in three publications: *The Rise of Islamic State: ISIS and the New Sunni Revolution*, by Patrick Cockburn; *The Islamic State: A Brief Introduction*, by Charles R. Lister, and *The ISIS Apocalypse: The History, Strategy and Doomsday Vision of the Islamic State*, by William McCants. Each of them traces the origins of the Islamic State from its earliest days when Abu Musab al Zarqawi founded it to its present incarnation under the leadership of an Islamic scholar, Abu Bakr al-Baghdadi and attempts to clarify the nature of ISIS.

Published first in February 2015, a few weeks after the attack on *Charlie Hebdo*, Cockburn's *The Rise of Islamic State* notes the complexities of the situation in the Middle

doi: 10.18278/gsis.1.2.10

East and excoriates the West for failing to understand them better. Cockburn, an award-winning journalist who has been covering the Middle East for more than 30 years, relies primarily on his own reporting and interviews as he develops his arguments. Cockburn believes that the war on terrorism is a failure because it failed to target two of the most important supporters of jihadism, Saudi Arabia and Pakistan. Because they are important American allies, Cockburn asserts, the United States has tried to avoid offending both. By doing so, he argues, the United States has contributed to the resurgence of jihadism in the Middle East. Cockburn also holds other states accountable, such as Great Britain and Turkey, for the success of ISIS. Saudi financing of jihadist groups has, he adds, contributed significantly to the violence between Shia and Sunni Muslims in Iraq and Syria.

Much of the book is focused on the Civil War in Syria. Cockburn argues that the West miscalculated in regard to the struggle there. This was partly due to a failure to understand the multiple conflicts taking place in that worn–torn state, but also to the assumption that Assad would be swiftly deposed. The inability of the original revolution against Assad's dictatorship to remove the Syrian president has led to the present stalemated situation, while the conflict itself has descended into a Shia–Sunni standoff and a revived "cold war" between Russia and the West in that part of the world. Cockburn describes the present situation in Syria as analogous to the Thirty Years' War in Europe, with the multiplicity of players involved unlikely to produce a peaceful resolution to the conflict any time soon. As a result, ISIS was able to take advantage of the Syrian Civil War in order to expand the territory under its control. The resolution of the situation in Syria and Iraq, Cockburn concludes, most likely rests with the United States, Russia, Saudi Arabia, and Iran, assuming that they can find a way to balance their competing interests in the region.

Ultimately, Cockburn sees a future filled with ferment, at least in the short term, for Syria and Iraq. The Civil War has no end in sight and the inability of the foreign states involved in the conflict to help bring a resolution to the fighting there have the people of Iraq and Syria at the mercy of events that may lead to the Islamic State becoming an "established geographic and political fact on the map."

In *The Islamic State: A Brief Introduction*, published in March 2015, Visiting Fellow at the Brookings Institution, Charles R.Lister describes the essential aspect of the organization as "lasting and expanding." Drawing mostly on secondary sources, with some primary ones, Lister describes this process as the fundamental *modus operandi* of the organization. He argues that despite its lack of Islamic legitimacy, the declaration of a caliphate by ISIS was an extremely audacious decision. Nonetheless, he asserts that ISIS will pose a significant challenge to the security of the Middle East and the international community, as a whole, for years and only a clear understanding of ISIS will lead to its ultimate defeat. Lister describes ISIS as "a qualitative evolution of the al-Qaeda model," but with a more professional military and the ability to have created a practical model for social governance that has been relatively successful, particularly in "unstable environments."

Militarily, the author describes the strategy of ISIS as having a dual nature. On one hand, the organization carries out mass casualty attacks in urban areas, targeting Shia, Alawi Muslims, and others, primary in civilian localities. And, as recent events have shown, ISIS has demonstrated the ability to carry out these types of attacks in Western Europe, as well as within Iraq, Syria, and other parts of the Middle East. The second aspect of the military strategy of ISIS is described as a process of attrition against its opponent's morale and capabilities. This requires a process of eroding the enemy's capacity to maintain the security of a targeted objective. The fall of Mosul, for example, was the result of carefully planned, intelligence-led operations that undermined the ability of Iraqi forces to control the periphery of the city while simultaneously carrying out covert operations designed to intimidate government officials, including the assassinations of the most experienced, senior officials. By doing so, the ability of government personnel to control the city was weakened and ISIS was able to create a shadow authority that operated covertly during daylight hours and, often, more openly at night. Alliances with other Sunni factions have also been an essential feature of ISIS military strategy.

Internally, Lister notes the professionalism of the senior leadership of ISIS, many of whom were former Iraqi military officers. ISIS has also taken the decision to operate as a nation-state, with a well-organized bureaucracy and the ability to generate revenue through taxation, extortion, and the sale of oil. ISIS has proved particularly adept at social media both for the promotion of its actions, especially through media exploitation and social networking, and for recruiting purposes. As for governance, Lister shows that the implementation of *sharia* law and the favoring of Sunni Muslims over all others is key, as is intimidation through the use of swift and brutal punishments.

How to defeat ISIS? Lister argues that defeating ISIS will take time and the leadership of local actors is supported by the West. It will also be necessary to treat ISIS as more than a terrorist organization. He calls for bolstering moderate opposition groups in Syria while persuading Russia and Iran to suppress military assistance to the Assad regime and joining in the effort to bring about a peaceful transition in Damascus. The existing agreements for the provision of military assistance to Iraq need to be honored, he believes, but future assistance must be made conditional. On a broad front, in both Syria and Iraq, Lister states that a strategy must be developed and implemented to weaken the strengths of ISIS—its revenue stream, effective leadership and command structure, mobile forces, use of social media, and the exploitation of regional stability. He notes that this will require an intensive intelligence collection, analysis effort, and improvements in key leader engagement especially at the local level. Lister argues that the "only real hope for neutralizing" the threat posed by ISIS it to correct the current political failures regionally and strengthen local opposition to it. While the international community will have to play "the vital role of facilitators, guarantors, and enforcers," Lister concludes that "it is the local players who will come to define the long-term fate of IS."

William McCants, Director of the Project on U.S. Relations with the Islamic World at the Brookings Institution, offers readers the kind of insights that may lead to the clear understanding of ISIS that Lister, his colleague at Brookings has called for. In *The ISIS Apocalypse: The History, Strategy and Doomsday Vision of the Islamic State*, McCants provides readers with a detailed analysis of the mission and message of ISIS. Proficient in Arabic and Islamic history and theology, McCants presents himself as uniquely qualified to dissect and evaluate the methods and message used by ISIS to attract followers and justify its actions. Backing up his claim, McCants cites numerous primary sources, including secret al-Qaida and ISIS documents written in Arabic to support his views.

The key to understanding ISIS, McCants argues, is in its vision—one that combines the long held dream of reviving the Islamic Empire with a vision of the coming End of Days. While these ideas may seem contradictory, the author points out that they became fashionable following the American invasion of Iraq in 2003. The outbreak of sectarian violence that followed soon after made a vision formerly held by fringe elements more appealing to a wider number of Muslims, Sunni in particular. The chaos unleashed by the events of the Arab Spring in 2012 only fueled belief in a coming apocalypse further. Polls conducted in the Middle East, McCants notes, revealed that 50 percent of Arabs responding believed that the Muslim savior, the Mahdi, would appear at any time, while reports of "End-Time heroes" being sighted and the increasing violence in Syria made doomsday prophecies more believable.

Like Cockburn and Lister, McCants traces the emergence of ISIS from its roots in earlier Islamic extremism, but in greater detail. He effectively outlines the increasing split between al-Qaida and what was to become the Islamic State, demonstrating that ISIS has moved far beyond the vision of Osama bin Laden in terms of the meaning and conduct of holy war. The contradiction between Bin Laden and ISIS is notable on several fronts, particularly in the use of violence and the establishment of a caliphate. While Bin Laden argued for winning popular support for al-Qaida before instituting a gradual implementation of *sharia*, ISIS prefers to use intimidation and brute force to establish control over the areas they have seized. Likewise, ISIS has ignored restrictions on the killing of Muslims, which earned several rebukes from Bin Laden and undoubtedly contributed to the eventual split between them. As McCants notes in his introduction, al-Qaida "tamped down messianic fervor and sought popular support," leaving the caliphate for the future. But ISIS fights and rules according to the Machiavellian principle that "It is far safer to be feared than loved." ISIS riles up messianic fervor, McCants writes, and they "want God's Kingdom now rather than later."

Despite the apocalyptic views embraced by ISIS, McCants cautions that these do not necessarily "demand rash and irrational behavior. "A severe religious theology is not incompatible with practical considerations." Even so, he notes, the political impact is still the same. What ISIS has created is a "brutal government at war with its neighbors." Will it modify its doctrine in order to survive in the long run, or will it cling to it in the belief that it "is destined to be a world-encompassing state." Whichever, McCants states that "the world can't afford to wait and find out."

Rejecting the presence of a large American military force to fight against ISIS because the move will be unpopular at home and the mission will not be successful, McCants also argues that this will also "absolve local governments from making the tough political choices required to end the Sunni disenfranchisement that fuels the insurgency." Continued use of air power to degrade the ability of ISIS to raise money and fight is recommended, along with the identification and careful use of proxies to combat ISIS. Ultimately, McCants believes that ISIS will be defeated, as no "modern jihadist statelet has provoked international intervention and survived." He warns, however, that the elimination of a jihadist statelet does not mean that the jihadists themselves will disappear. As long as political instability exists in the Middle East jihadism will continue in some form.

Something missing, not only from McCants' work, but also from the books by Cockburn and Lister, is more attention to the adept use of social media by ISIS. While not entirely overlooked, the subject might have been examined in greater depth. The skill ISIS has shown in producing technically excellent videos highlighting its successes (and atrocities), and its adroit use of social media to promulgate its theological and ideological views in order to inspire and recruit fighters and supporters that deserves more attention than it receives in these books. Setting aside the terrorism component of ISIS, an examination of how ISIS has used social media for recruiting purposes alone would have added a much needed dimension to each book.

Each author also notes the importance of local elements in bringing the current conflict to a resolution. While the major powers all have interests to protect in this part of the world, it is evident to all the writers that a true settlement of the present situation will have to involve the nations of the Middle East, not only as participants but as leaders in the process. Exactly how this will be accomplished, however, remains elusive as the recommendations each offers for defeating ISIS suggest.

Together, this trio of books provides insightful and disturbing analyses of ISIS. But the question of what, exactly, ISIS is remains unanswered. The November attacks in Paris, the shootings in San Bernardino in December, and the Brussels bombings all were inspired by or conducted by cells or individuals loyal to the Islamic State. Yet ISIS has also used conventional military tactics to carve out what is, at least, a proto state from Syrian and Iraqi territory. At this point, ISIS seems to be a hybrid—part terrorist organization and part military insurgency, flexible enough to use violence in a variety of ways in pursuit of its ultimate goal. Each of these authors, taken together, paint a portrait of an organization that has used a military insurgency to carve out a geographic stronghold, while demonstrating the ability to attack its enemies in their respective homelands with terrorist violence. ISIS rules through fear and brutality in the regions it controls, while using terrorist tactics to try and intimidate the populations of those nations that oppose it. This forces those combatting ISIS to develop strategies and tactics that are designed to stabilize the situation in the Middle East, particularly in Syria and Iraq, while also applying counterterrorism resources to defend their respective homelands. Interestingly, each author focuses on the former rather than the latter as they consider methods that might lead to the defeat of ISIS. That might be due to the fact that ISIS directed or inspired terrorist attacks on the West began to take place mostly after each of these books was published. More than two-dozen terrorist events related to ISIS have taken place since the announcement of the Caliphate in June 2014; the majority of them occurred in 2015, culminating in the Brussels bombings in January.

This raises the peril of publishing while events continue to unfold. The rise of ISIS and its declaration of a Caliphate naturally led these writers to concentrate on the military insurgency taking place in Syria and Iraq, and less on the potential for terrorist attacks. That is understandable, given the events of the period in which these books appeared. And, Lister and McCants have continued to develop their ideas both on the Brookings web site and elsewhere. Cockburn likewise continues to comment on ISIS in various sources. Even so, each of these books and the views expressed by their authors run the danger of becoming out of date rather quickly. Nonetheless, taken together, these three books provide an excellent introduction into the nature of ISIS. They offer a useful survey of the Islamic State's theological justification for its actions, how it operates and the threat it presents to the world. All are worth reading and the time taken to absorb the ideas presented in them will be worthwhile.

Gregory Moore, Ph.D.
Notre Dame College, South Euclid, Ohio

www.ingramcontent.com/pod-product-compliance
Lightning Source LLC
Chambersburg PA
CBHW081649270326
41933CB00018B/3404